THE STARTUP FOUNDER'S

—— GUIDE TO ——

DIGITAL

MARKETING

THE STARTUP FOUNDER'S GUIDE TO

DIGITAL MARKETING

PRAMOD MALOO

HARPER
BUSINESS

An Imprint of HarperCollins Publishers

First published in India by Harper Business 2025
An imprint of HarperCollins *Publishers*
HarperCollins *Publishers* India, Cyber City,
Building 10-A, Gurugram, Haryana – 122002, India
www.harpercollins.co.in

2 4 6 8 10 9 7 5 3 1

P-ISBN: 978-93-7307-142-8
E-ISBN: 978-93-7307-626-3

Typeset in 11/14.7 Adobe Garamond Pro
by HarperCollins *Publishers* India Pvt. Ltd

Printed and bound at
Replika Press Pvt. Ltd.

HarperCollins *Publishers*, Macken House, 39/40 Mayor Street Upper,
Dublin 1, D01 C9W8, Ireland

*To Kaira and Mahiera—the two brightest stars of my life.
Your love and laughter is the fuel that powers my life.*

The detailed notes pertaining to this book are available on the HarperCollins website. Scan this QR code to access the same.

Contents

SECTION III: SLAY THE GAME

Introduction

Marketing in the Digital Age Is a Totally Different Ballgame

TODAY'S START-UPS HOLD THE POWER TO TRANSFORM the way we live, disrupt traditional business models, and create lasting impact. As the pace of innovation accelerates and competition becomes fiercer, effective marketing—especially in the digital realm— is the critical differentiator between those who thrive and those who struggle to find their footing.

This book aims to help you navigate the digital landscape and achieve scalable, sustainable growth by providing you strategic clarity and practical know-how.

All of us understand that success today is not merely about having a brilliant idea; it is about playing the business game skilfully. In this book, we will explore essential strategies, learn how to play with finesse in a competitive arena, and ultimately slay the game, emerging as a formidable contender in the modern marketplace.

As former Unilever CMO Keith Weed said, 'We should no longer be talking about "digital marketing", but marketing in a digital world.'[1]

There is a fundamental shift in how businesses approach marketing. Earlier, digital marketing was seen as a separate, specialized discipline— focused on online tactics like social media, SEO, and email campaigns. However, today's world is inherently digital, making all marketing inherently digital too.

Consumers seamlessly move between physical and digital touchpoints—browsing products online before purchasing in-store, scanning QR codes, or engaging with brands via AI-powered chatbots. This convergence means marketing is no longer about choosing between 'traditional' and 'digital'—it's about creating an integrated 'phygital' experience across all channels.

Brands must shift from siloed digital strategies to a customer-first approach, where marketing leverages real-time data, automation, and AI to personalize interactions. Companies like Amazon and Nike exemplify this by blending online and offline experiences, using data-driven insights to drive engagement and conversions.

In essence, marketing in a digital world means embracing technology, agility, and customer-centricity at every level—not just as an add-on but as the core of modern marketing. Businesses that fail to adapt will struggle to stay relevant in today's interconnected ecosystem.

Before diving into the strategies that will propel your start-up forward, it's essential to first set up the framework to get an overview of the overall approach.

The following strategic framework/gameplan will shape your digital marketing approach, help you make informed decisions, align your strategies with your start-up's vision, and ultimately, unlock the full potential of digital marketing to drive your business to new heights.

The Strategic Game Plan

The strategic game plan has been divided into three broad heads:

1. Learn the game
2. Play the game
3. Slay the game

In short, happy gaming folks!

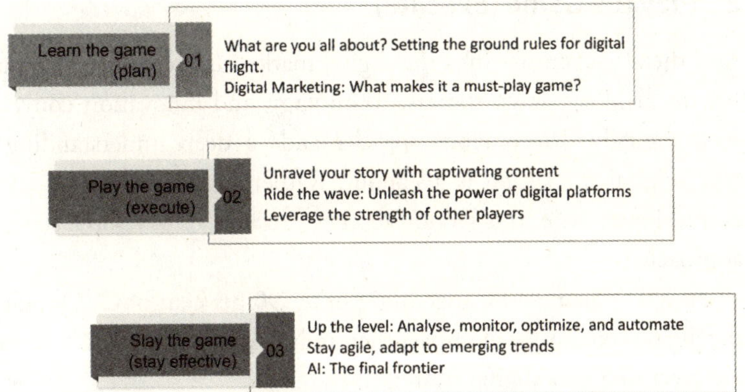

1. Learn the Game (Plan)

We begin by walking you through the foundational pillars of any successful venture.

- **What are you all about? Setting the ground rules for digital flight**

  We visit some fundamental aspects of business to underline why establishing a relevant mission and vision is pivotal for guiding decisions and forming a cohesive brand identity, and how understanding the competition and projecting your unique value proposition (UVP) is so crucial. While these may appear very basic ideas, not having them in place can definitely be detrimental to your business.

- **What makes digital marketing a must-play game?**

  Mastering the game of digital marketing has numerous positives, from precise targeting to measurable impact; from driving innovation to attaining cross-border reach; and of course, benefitting from cost-effective marketing solutions. In short, it is imperative, impeccable, and irresistible.

2. Play the Game (Execute)

And then, we venture into the digital marketing arena—the dynamic playing field where customers, technology, and innovation converge. This digitally driven landscape demands a deep understanding of what digital marketing is all about. Rather than haphazardly trying everything at once, this section teaches you how to develop a strategic approach.

As MIT Sloan and Capgemini put it, '90 per cent of CEOs believe the digital economy will impact their industry, but less than 15 per cent are executing on a digital strategy'.[2]

➤ Create Your Story with Captivating Content

This is all about creating a consistent and compelling brand narrative that resonates with the target audience. 'Stories create connections, and connections build trust, ultimately transforming customers into loyal advocates for a brand, helping you create more connections.'[3]

You will learn more about how to create captivating content using the S.T.O.R.Y. framework:

- o   Start with your audience
- o   Tell your brand story
- o   Offer your unique selling proposition
- o   Resonate emotionally
- o   Yield action

➤ Unleash the Power of Digital Platforms

In this section, you will learn about the most important and relevant paid and organic marketing campaigns and channels. These platforms provide traffic, visibility, engagement, community, leads, interaction, sales and so much more.

- **Search engine optimization (SEO): A marathon, not a sprint**

  Involves SEO strategies to rank higher on search engine results pages (SERPs) and drive organic traffic to your website. The *five SEO sprints* will help you dominate the game of search engine domination:

  - The digital footprint
  - The content ecosystem
  - The authority accelerator
  - The technical tune-up
  - The competitive edge

- **Social media: The new-age hook**

  This is the new-age drug of the 21st century. It is becoming next to impossible to not check Instagram (IG), Facebook (FB), X (formerly Twitter), and LinkedIn (LI) throughout our active hours. As an advertiser, it is *the* place to promote your brand. You will learn how to choose and use the social media platforms based on goals, target group buyer persona etc. It entails sharing content consistently and engaging with followers. You will learn more about how to choose wisely and make the most out of these social media platforms using the L.I.F.T. and C.A.S.T. frameworks.

L.I.F.T.	C.A.S.T.
Leverage	Clarity
Inspire	Audience
Focus	Scope
Track	Time

- **Leveraging advertising powerhouses: Google and Meta ads**

  Using platforms like Google Ads and social media ads (Facebook, Instagram, LinkedIn) to reach the target audience. Want to emerge as the winner in the game of return-on-investment (ROI) from paid performance? Our time-tested T.R.A.C.E. framework will help you do so.

  - Target
  - Reach
  - Act
  - Convert
  - Evaluate

- **Retargeting and remarketing: Recapturing the leaked opportunities**

  Using the power of remarketing and retargeting campaigns to re-engage with your existing customers, and to continuously hammer potential ones about your products and services. The L.O.O.P. framework will guide you to optimize results from retargeting and remarketing.

  - Listen
  - Offer
  - Optimize
  - Persist

- **Connect and converse with WhatsApp and email**

  The advent of messenger apps is a great boon for marketing. This would involve making use of WhatsApp, Facebook Messenger, Telegram, etc.

The F.R.I.E.N.D. framework is your friend while navigating through easy yet effective marketing to reach maximum numbers at most affordable pricing.

- o   Find
- o   Reach out
- o   Inform
- o   Engage
- o   Nurture
- o   Develop

➢ **Leverage Strength of Other Players**

▪ **Master influencer marketing**

This involves collaborating with micro-influencers or industry partners to tap into their audiences, build credibility and drive engagement. You will learn about the M.A.T.C.H. framework to help you master the game of influencer marketing.

- o   Mission alignment
- o   Audience fit
- o   Trustworthiness
- o   Content quality
- o   History of performance

▪ **Building your digital PR engine: A foolproof system**

Digital PR focuses on managing how your business is represented and perceived online. From fixing a damaged reputation to building credibility in your industry, from positioning yourself as a thought leader to creating trust for your new product, digital PR and communication can do it all.

We have successfully helped our clients excel in the branding game using the C.L.E.A.R. framework on digital platforms.

- o   Clarify the narrative
- o   Leverage media channels
- o   Engage authentically
- o   Activate campaigns
- o   Review and refine

- **Moving up to the marketplaces**

Marketplaces provide start-ups with the infrastructure, visibility, and customer base they need to scale without having to invest heavily in marketing, logistics, or platform development. Leveraging these established ecosystems can help businesses grow faster and more efficiently.

The Visibility Pyramid is a framework we've used for years to help SMBs succeed on online marketplaces. There are six levels, including zero.

- o   Level 0: Effective listing
- o   Level 1: Platform SEO
- o   Level 2: Platform advertising
- o   Level 3: Customer reviews and ratings
- o   Level 4: Off-platform marketing
- o   Level 5: Brand authority

- **Revamp your reach: Leveraging OTTs, webinars, and more**

As a start-up founder, you pour your heart and soul into your digital marketing plan. You tick all the right boxes—optimize for SEO, maintain a consistent social media presence, run paid ads, and analyse metrics. Yet, the growth seems negligible, and not how you expected. That's when you need to consider these advanced marketing channels:

- o Over-the-top (OTT) marketing
- o Affiliate marketing
- o Podcast marketing
- o Digital out-of-home (DOOH) advertising
- o Webinar marketing
- o Push notification marketing

- **Tailored sectoral strategies for industry-specific success**

  The key to success lies in understanding that every sector requires a slight change in tactics. So, we need to understand the requirements of some major sectors to appreciate how the tactics used undergo some changes.

3. Slay the Game (Winning Moves)

You will see how to scale and automate your operations without losing the personal touch that differentiates you. We will explore the strategies to monitor and analyse performance, and continuously innovate to ride new trends. Finally, we get to the final frontier—artificial intelligence (AI)—and address its transformative impact. From AI tools and agents that can streamline your business processes, to predictive analytics, to emerging AI platforms (that empower smaller businesses by democratizing cutting-edge technology), we help you understand how to make AI work for your business.

- **Metrics matter: Analyse, monitor, optimize**

  This means monitoring the performance of all digital marketing efforts using data-driven analysis; setting up Google Analytics, social media analytics, and email marketing tools to track and measure campaign effectiveness.

- **Automate to elevate: Automation for growth**

  As the start-up grows, you need to automate the marketing efforts wherever possible, so as to scale effectively. This would involve:

  - Email automation: Using tools like Mailchimp and ActiveCampaign to send automated drip campaigns.

  - Chatbots: Implementing chatbots on the website for real-time customer support and engagement.

  - Ad campaigns: Automation of retargeting and paid campaigns based on user behaviour.

- **Adapt to emerging trends**

  For a start-up, this means staying responsive to changes in technology, consumer behaviour, industry dynamics, and market conditions, to maintain competitiveness and growth. Start-ups, unlike established companies, often operate in fast-moving environments, and their success depends on their ability to identify, assess, and quickly incorporate new trends into their strategies.

  This imperative is all about future-proofing your business, and would include:

  - Responding to competitor movements
  - Adapting to consumer behaviour trends

     o   Leveraging emerging technology

     o   Experimentation and innovation, etc.

- **AI: The final frontier**

  Artificial intelligence is reshaping marketing in ways most businesses still don't fully understand. This book will be incomplete without a look at the necessary AI tools to make your digital marketing journey quick, easy and productive. In this chapter, all the relevant tools have been categorized under ideation and execution level, and further, on the basis of broad functionalities. You will get to know all the tools to make your life easy—from ideation to content creation; from image to video editing/creation; from social media management to ads management; from email marketing to customer engagement and more.

How This Book Will Help You

- **Actionable framework:** Rather than just theory, we provide a clear pathway—learn, play, and slay—so you can methodically build, refine, and excel in your marketplace.

- **Real-world insights**: You find references illustrating how each principle applies in the real world. You learn how established players used different strategies and tactics to grow exponentially.

- **Strategic and practical:** Each chapter offers step-by-step guidance, from setting your vision and brand story, to orchestrating advanced online campaigns and embracing AI solutions.

- **Future-focused:** Today's business environment is ever-evolving; we focus on cultivating agility and innovation, highlighting how AI will redefine the competitive landscape.

Now that we've got an overview of the strategic roadmap/gameplan for your brand's digital marketing, it's time to start on the action plan, which will play a pivotal role in making your business a long-term player in this game. Arm yourself with the insights and strategies within these pages, and you'll be poised to slay the game with agility, creativity, and unstoppable momentum.

SECTION I

Learn the Game

1

What Are You All About? Setting the Ground Rules for Digital Flight

1.1 The Power of Brand Perception

BRAND PERCEPTION CAN MAKE OR BREAK A START-UP. People align with brands that reflect their own values, forming deep emotional connections. When customers trust a brand, they defend it even in the face of setbacks. Conversely, brands with weak messaging are scrutinized and easily dismissed.

A start-up's strength lies in its innovation, agility, and ability to challenge old ways. Establishing a clear identity—rooted in mission, vision, and values—is crucial for creating a brand that resonates and scales. However, as businesses grow and markets shift, start-ups must periodically revisit these fundamentals to ensure continued relevance and impact.

1.2 Defining Your Brand Identity

Branding expert David Brier said, 'If you don't give the market the story to talk about, they'll define your brand's story for you.'[1] This is especially true for start-ups, where differentiation is key. Your brand identity stems from three fundamental pillars:

- **Mission (why you exist)**: Your purpose. For example, a renewable energy start-up's mission could be to make sustainable energy accessible to all.

- **Vision (where you're going):** The long-term impact you strive for. For example, a retailer might envision having flagship outlets in major cities.

- **Values (what guides you)**: Core principles shaping your culture and decisions. For example, a start-up prioritizing transparency ensures openness in pricing and operations.

- **Start-up Categories That Mastered Brand Clarity**

Here are some hypothetical examples of brand clarity across different verticals:

Tech start-up (AI and machine learning)

- **Mission**: Solve complex global problems using AI-driven solutions.

- **Vision**: A world where AI streamlines efficiency, freeing people for creativity.

- **Values**: Innovation, transparency, and collaboration.

Health and wellness start-up (Mental health app)

- **Mission**: Make mental health support accessible and stigma-free.

- **Vision**: A world where emotional well-being is as prioritized as physical health.

- **Values**: Empathy, accessibility, and continuous innovation.

A start-up's ability to revisit and refine these pillars is essential for staying relevant in evolving markets. Your audience must understand exactly *why you exist* and *what problem you solve*.

- **Why Start-ups Need to Revisit Their Brand Strategy**

A start-up's mission, vision, and brand positioning are not static—they should evolve with the market, consumer expectations, and internal business growth. Companies that fail to adapt risk becoming irrelevant.

Netflix's evolution

Netflix started as a DVD rental service but adapted its mission and brand identity to remain relevant in the digital era. By shifting from renting DVDs to streaming, and later into content production, it continuously refined its brand to align with changing consumer preferences and technology trends. Today, Netflix is synonymous with global entertainment because of its ability to pivot and redefine its core value proposition.

Paytm's expansion

Originally a mobile recharge platform, Paytm redefined its mission as it grew, evolving into a comprehensive digital payments ecosystem. Recognizing market demand, it expanded into financial services, making digital transactions accessible to millions. By revisiting and refining its mission, vision, and values, Paytm ensured it stayed ahead in a competitive landscape.

1.3 The Role of Branding in Start-ups

A brand is more than a logo or product—it's an experience, a promise, and a reputation. In today's fast-paced digital world, start-ups must differentiate themselves through brand storytelling and customer engagement.

- **What Branding Really Does**

  Branding is your start-up's most valuable intangible asset. Iconic brands like Apple and Tesla don't just sell products; they sell experiences and ideologies. Apple positions itself as sleek and empowering; Tesla as revolutionary and futuristic; Airbnb as warm and personal.

- **Why Branding Matters More Than Ever for Start-ups**

  o **It cuts through the noise**

  In crowded markets, a well-defined brand helps customers choose you over competitors. Without strong branding, your start-up is just another option rather than the preferred choice.

  o **It builds long-term trust**

  Customers are drawn to consistency and authenticity. Take beauty brand Glossier, for example. By engaging directly with its audience, encouraging user-generated content, and prioritizing transparency, the brand built a dedicated community that drove its success.

  o **It creates a scalable growth engine**

  Zomato started as a restaurant review platform before evolving into a food delivery giant. Its ability to listen to user feedback and refine its brand positioning allowed it to scale rapidly while staying relevant.

1.4 Understanding Your Target Audience

A start-up succeeds by solving problems for a specific audience. Identifying and deeply understanding your customers ensures effective messaging and product-market fit.

- **Steps to Defining Your Target Market**

  - **Identify core customers**: Who benefits the most from your solution? For example, fitness enthusiasts for a plant-based protein brand.

  - **Develop buyer personas**: Define demographics, pain points, and motivations.

  - **Conduct market research**: Surveys, social listening, and competitor analysis help refine messaging.

For example, Zomato saw the gap in restaurant discovery, and positioned itself as the go-to platform for reviews, eventually transitioning into food delivery based on market demand.

1.5 Competitive Analysis and Finding Your Edge

Rather than copying competitors, analyse them to identify gaps. What are they missing? How can your start-up uniquely solve customer problems?

- **Positioning Your Unique Value Proposition (UVP)**

  Your UVP is what makes you stand out. It's not just what you do, but *why* customers should choose you.

  - **Tesla**: 'Accelerating the world's transition to sustainable energy.'

  - **Slack**: 'Be less busy.'

  - **Airbnb**: 'Belong anywhere.'

1.6 Conclusion

Start-ups are about innovation, problem-solving, and new approaches to old challenges. Branding isn't just about visibility; it's about relevance, trust, and long-term impact. Revisiting mission, vision, and values is *not just a one-time exercise*, but a *continuous process* that keeps your business adaptable, scalable, and future-ready.

With a clear *mission, vision, values* and *UVP*, your start-up won't just exist—it will *thrive* in a competitive digital world.

Since the ground rules are now in place, let's take a look at the strategic advantages of digital marketing, so that you can understand the substantive impacts that you can aim for.

2

Digital Marketing: What Makes It a Must-Play Game for Start-ups?

YOU'VE BUILT SOMETHING FROM NOTHING. YOU KNOW the sacrifices, the long nights, and the relentless pursuit of success. But the marketing landscape has shifted—what once worked no longer guarantees results. The solution? Adapt and thrive in the digital era.

The New Reality

Technology has revolutionized business operations. Internet isn't just a tool—it's the foundation of modern commerce. Every customer journey now moves between online and offline touchpoints. For start-ups, this presents an opportunity: with the right digital strategies, even a small business can compete with industry giants. But do you have the mindset, strategy, and execution plan to make digital work for you?

Why Digital Marketing Is Non-Negotiable for Start-ups

2.1 Levels the Playing Field

Big budgets once ruled marketing, but now a single viral post can propel a start-up into the limelight. Dollar Shave Club, with a witty low-budget YouTube video, reached millions and disrupted a billion-dollar industry. With smart content, any start-up can gain massive traction.

2.2 Precise Targeting and Measurable Impact

Traditional marketing casts a wide net, hoping for results. Digital marketing ensures precision. Airbnb, in its early days, used Facebook ads and Google AdWords to target travellers searching for budget accommodations. Tracking metrics like click-through rate (CTR) and return on ad spend (ROAS), it optimized every ad dollar, transforming from a start-up to a global leader.

2.3 Building Relationships and Trust

Consumers want connection and authenticity. Glossier built a beauty empire by engaging customers on social media, crowdsourcing product ideas, and showcasing real user experiences. Its direct, customer-first approach fostered brand loyalty and exponential growth.

2.4 Agility: The Start-up Advantage

Start-ups can pivot quickly. Dunzo, a hyperlocal delivery start-up, adapted its marketing during COVID-19, emphasizing contactless deliveries and community-driven campaigns. By leveraging real-time consumer data, it scaled operations and reinforced customer trust.

2.5 Cost-Effective Marketing

Every rupee counts for start-ups. Zappos, an online retailer, focused on SEO, targeted ads and conversion tracking instead of expensive traditional media. This allowed it to maximize ROI and scale effectively without large marketing budgets.

2.6 Global Reach with Local Precision

Start-ups can scale globally while customizing efforts for local markets. Spotify mastered this by pairing global brand campaigns with region-specific playlists and language-targeted ads. This dual approach fuelled its worldwide success.

2.7 Driving Innovation and Growth

Data-driven marketing fosters innovation. Lenskart transformed eyewear sales in India with its 3D Try-On tool, promoted heavily via digital channels. Its ability to integrate data, refine offerings, and seamlessly blend online and offline experiences contributed to rapid expansion.

Conclusion

Love it or hate it, digital marketing is here to stay. It's not just an option—it's your start-up's *lifeline*. Understanding and leveraging digital tools can mean the difference between obscurity and dominance. The question is no longer *if* you should embrace digital marketing, but *how well* you play the game. Let's get started.

Now that we are clear on the critical importance of this game, let's start playing!

Beginning with your content—how to craft content that captivates your audience and keeps them hooked onto your brand?

SECTION II

Play the Game

3

Unfolding Content Marketing: Creating Compelling Content

'MARKETING IS NO LONGER ABOUT THE STUFF THAT you make, but about the stories you tell,' said Seth Godin, founder of Squidoo (acquired by Hubpages).[1]

As a business owner, you might feel like posting product pictures on social media is enough to stay visible. It's quick, familiar, and feels manageable, right? Then you scroll through your social media feeds, and you can't help but notice the competition: brands that seem to effortlessly craft viral videos, weave compelling stories, and rack up thousands of engagements. This leaves you wondering, what are they doing differently? What's their secret sauce?

Getting Noticed: The Biggest Challenge Faced by Start-ups

Kaarigar, a small local handicrafts business in Rajasthan, was struggling to stand out in the crowded market. Despite producing high-quality products, it couldn't differentiate itself from competitors who sold similar items at lower prices. Most customers viewed Kaarigar's products as generic, and the business faced stiff competition from both local shops and online platforms. Without a unique brand identity, it struggled to attract loyal customers and build a sustainable online presence.

The business realized that simply listing products online wasn't enough. Customers wanted more than just products; they wanted a reason to connect emotionally with the brand. The solution was to tell the *stories behind the artisans* who crafted the products. By sharing the cultural heritage, traditional techniques, and personal stories of the artisans, the business could appeal to the emotional side of customers and show the value behind each item.

Kaarigar launched an Instagram and Facebook campaign featuring:

- Short videos of artisans working on traditional techniques passed down through generations.

- Story posts highlighting the struggles, expertise, and dedication of the craftspeople.

- Content that showcased the rich cultural history of Rajasthan behind each product.

This storytelling approach helped build a deeper connection with the audience. People didn't just see the handicrafts as products, but as part of Indian heritage and the lives of the artisans. The business saw an increase in online engagement, higher product demand, and a more loyal customer base willing to pay for authentic, handmade goods, because they connected with the stories behind them. *Stories win the day.*

By sharing the stories of the people and heritage behind them, Kaarigar was able to stand out in the market and build lasting relationships with customers. Storytelling transformed the brand and positioned it not just another handicrafts store, but a curator of cultural tradition.

3.1 Success Through Storytelling

Start-ups face constant challenges, like breaking through price-sensitive markets, simplifying complex products, or competing with industry giants. Storytelling is one of the most effective ways to tackle these issues. Let's look at how some brands used storytelling to rise above the competition.

- **Building Trust in a Price-Sensitive Market**

  Paytm earned consumer trust during the 2016 demonetization in India by sharing real-life stories of small shop owners and individuals using their digital wallets to overcome cash shortages. These stories emphasized reliability and real-world impact, helping Paytm become a household name.

Image source: ETBSI[2]

- **Differentiating in a Saturated Market**

  Chumbak's founders shared how travel and Indian culture inspired their designs, creating an emotional connection with young, urban Indians. This focus on storytelling gave Chumbak a distinctive identity in the competitive lifestyle market.

Image source: Whizky.com[3]

- **Communicating Value of a Complex Product**

Freshworks highlighted customer success stories to explain the benefits of its Software-as-a-Service (SaaS) products to small businesses. Through relatable case studies and webinars, it showed tangible results, making its software approachable and credible.

Source: People Matters[4]

- **Competing with Big Brands on a Limited Budget**

BoAt tapped into influencer marketing and shared energetic, youth-focused content on Instagram and YouTube. Highlighting customer stories ('BoAtheads') helped position their affordable products as aspirational, building a loyal community without big budgets.

Image source: Bhattacharya, 2022[5]

▪ Gaining Traction with a Niche Audience

Blue Tokai connected with coffee enthusiasts by sharing its farm-to-cup journey. Through stories about ethical sourcing, Indian coffee farmers, and the roasting process, it built a loyal customer base of artisanal coffee lovers.

Image source: Blue Tokai Coffee Roasters Instagram photo.[6]

3.2 Content Marketing: An Overview

This overview encompasses all the aspects of content marketing, from the basis/framework, to the various types of content, to the content style and tips which have to be used to create captivating content.

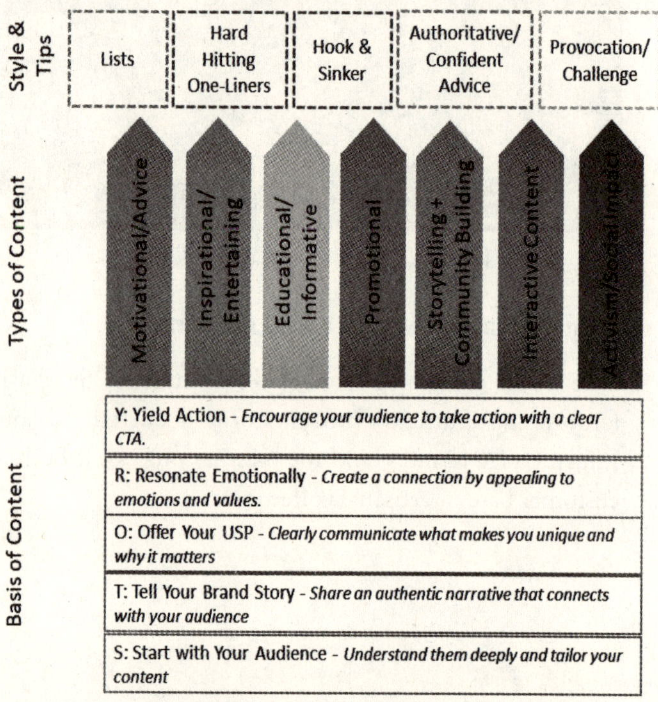

Image source: Author's illustration

If you want to connect with your audience and see real growth, it takes more than just posting the basics. Let's now show you exactly how to do this with a clear, actionable plan that works, using the S.T.O.R.Y. framework.

3.3 S.T.O.R.Y. Framework for Creating Captivating Content

3.3.1 S: Start with Your Audience

Your content should revolve around your audience's interests and pain points. The majority of your consumers would appreciate a piece of content that resonates with their problem, makes them feel seen or heard, or make them able to relate to the brand in some way.

Eventually, they connect with the brand at a deeper level, and convert to a loyal fanbase. This foundation will become your survival kit amid all the up-and-coming brands with flashy noise.

The more you know about the audience's interests, challenges, and preferences, the better you can craft content that speaks directly to them.

- **Know your audience**: The first step in creating captivating content is to deeply understand your target audience. Research their demographics, interests, pain points, and what drives them.

- **Tailor your message**: Use language, tone, and references that resonate with them. Think about how your content can solve their problems, meet their needs, or provide them with value.

Steps:

- o **Research:** Use surveys, social media insights, or customer feedback to learn about your audience's demographics (age, location, profession) and psychographics (values, interests, lifestyle).

- o **Segment your audience:** Not all your audience will be the same. Segment them based on factors like age, purchasing behaviour, or pain points. This helps tailor content specifically for each group.

- ○ **Speak their language:** Use the tone, style, and terminology that aligns with how your audience communicates. Whether it's formal, casual, humorous, or authoritative—make sure it feels familiar to them.

When your content speaks directly to their needs, they are more likely to engage, trust, and take action.

3.3.2 T: Tell Your Brand Story

- **Authenticity**: Share the story behind your brand. What inspired its creation? What challenges has it overcome? This helps humanize your brand and make it relatable.

- **Narrative style**: Craft your content like a story, with a clear beginning, middle, and end. A compelling narrative draws people in and keeps them engaged.

Some ideas focusing on brand story:

- ○ **Origin story video:** Create a video that shares your brand's journey, highlighting key milestones and the vision driving your brand.

- ○ **Founder's interview:** Conduct an interview with your founder or CEO to showcase the motivations and values shaping your brand. This humanizes your business and builds audience connection.

- ○ **Timeline infographic:** Design an infographic that visually depicts your brand's evolution, including major milestones and contributions.

3.3.3 O: Offer Your Unique Value Proposition

- **Highlight what sets you apart**: Why does UVP matter? Highlighting it is what makes your brand different from competitors. Whether it's your innovative product, exceptional customer service, or sustainability efforts, make sure to highlight this in your content.

- **Be clear and specific**: Use concrete examples or data points to support your claims.

Some content ideas focusing on UVP:

- o **Product showcase:** Develop content that highlights the unique features and benefits of your products or services.

- o **Comparison content:** Create articles or videos that compare your offerings with your competitors', emphasizing what sets your brand apart.

- o **Behind-the-scenes:** Share behind-the-scenes content showcasing your production process or quality control, emphasizing your commitment to excellence.

3.3.4 R: Resonate Emotionally

As Brandon Stanton, founder of Humans of New York, said, 'The most pivotal moments in people's lives revolve around emotions. Emotions make stories powerful.'

- **Create an emotional connection**: Content that stirs emotions is more likely to be shared and remembered. Whether it's through humour, empathy, or inspiration, focus on how you can make your audience *feel* something.

- **Align with values**: Show your audience that you understand their struggles, dreams, or aspirations. Use stories, testimonials, or visual content to make this connection more impactful.

Building an emotional connection with your audience is key to fostering brand loyalty and trust.

Why it matters:

- ○ **Enhanced brand loyalty:** When you connect emotionally with your customers, they are more likely to remain loyal, even when they have a choice of competing alternatives.

- ○ **Trust and credibility:** Emotional connections also foster trust, making customers more likely to believe in and support your brand.

- ○ **Brand advocacy:** Emotionally engaged customers often become your brand advocates, promoting your products or services through word-of-mouth, sharing their positive experiences.

How to create an emotional connection:

- ○ **Understand your audience:** Conduct research to understand your target audience's values, needs, and pain points (we have already gone over this point in section 3.3.1).

- ○ **Tell authentic stories:** Share genuine, relatable stories that resonate with your audience's experiences.

- ○ **Highlight shared values:** Emphasize values that your brand and audience share, such as sustainability or social causes.

- ○ **Create engaging content:** Use storytelling, visuals, and narratives that evoke emotions like joy, nostalgia, or inspiration.

- ○ **Share customer success stories:** Showcase real-life examples of customers benefiting from your products, enhancing credibility.

- ○ **Humanize your brand:** Introduce the people behind your brand—they may be artisans, workers, farmers or employees. This will make your business more relatable.

o **Utilize user-generated content:** Share content created by your customers, demonstrating their loyalty and real-world use of your products.

A great example of tapping human emotions is the Google ad titled 'Reunion', the story of two friends separated during the Partition of India and Pakistan, who found each other through Google.

Creating an emotional connection is an ongoing process that requires empathy, authenticity, and a genuine commitment to understanding and meeting your customers' emotional needs. When you do it effectively, it leads to lasting and mutually beneficial relationships with your audience.

3.3.5 Y: Yield Action

The ultimate goal of your content is to drive action—whether it's signing up for a newsletter, making a purchase, or sharing the content with others. Every piece of content should guide your audience toward taking the next step.

- **Clear call-to-action (CTA):** Always include a clear, concise CTA that tells the audience what to do next, whether it's signing up for a newsletter, making a purchase, or following your social media accounts. For examples, 'buy now', 'sign up today', 'learn more', or 'follow us for updates'.

- **Create urgency:** Encourage immediate action by using 'limited-time offer!' or 'only a few spots left!'

- **Offer incentives:** Provide rewards such as discounts, freebies, or exclusive content to motivate action. This makes the decision to act feel more rewarding.

3.4 Measuring Content Marketing Effectiveness

Content marketing helps you establish your brand and occupy the mind-space of your target audience. If done properly, it builds brand authority and creates trust. Further, it helps in search engine optimization (SEO) and also complements other marketing efforts.

- ### Which Key Performance Indicators (KPIs) to Track?

    You can measure KPIs in multiple ways, depending on the platform and objectives. For instance, you can consider website traffic like unique visitors, page views, bounce rate, average session duration by a user etc.; or engagement KPIs such as likes, shares, comments, mentions on social media; or ROI/ conversion KPIs like cost per lead, customer lifetime value, cost per acquisition, or revenue growth metrics.

To get the best out of content marketing, you need to mix content types—educational, entertaining, informative, storytelling, promotional, etc. A content calendar ensures consistent posting. Remember, all marketing is about storytelling, and digital technology amplifies this fundamental principle. Here's a streamlined strategy for success.

3.5 Social Media Post Categories with Tactics and Examples

Creating captivating content is an art that improves with practice.

Keep experimenting and refining your skills, and stay attuned to your audience's needs—this will enable you to consistently improve your content marketing game and produce content that resonates with your target group.

These are the eight most powerful broad content styles, along with examples.

3.5.1 Motivational/Advice

Purpose: Motivate or provide actionable tips to get the audience into action mode.

Tactics:

- o **Hooks**: Start with questions or challenges.

  'What's stopping you from achieving your goals today?'

- o **One-liners**: Deliver a punchy, motivational phrase.

  'Every expert was once a beginner. Start now!'

- o **Formulas**: Problem > Action > Result.

  'Struggling with procrastination? Try the 5-minute rule: Commit to just 5 minutes of work, and watch the momentum build!'

Examples:

- o **Fitness**: 'You're only 1 workout away from a better mood. Start today!'

- o **Entrepreneurship**: 'Turn "I wish" into "I will". Your journey starts now!'

- o **Education**: 'Study tip: Review your notes within 24 hours for better retention!'

3.5.2 Inspirational

Purpose: Share uplifting messages to inspire positivity.

Tactics:

- o **Quotes**: Pair inspiring words with beautiful visuals.

  '"The best way to predict the future is to create it"—Peter Drucker.'

- o **Visuals**: Nature or serene imagery with soft typography.

- o **Story Hooks**: Personal or relatable journeys.

  'I failed 3 times before I finally succeeded. Here's what I learned.'

Examples:

- o **Health:** 'Your mental health matters as much as your physical health. Take a break when you need it.'
- o **Business:** 'Every big idea started with someone daring to dream.'
- o **Travel:** 'Not all who wander are lost. Keep exploring!'

3.5.3 Educational/Informative + Debunking Myths

Purpose: Provide knowledge, tips, or correct misconceptions.

Tactics:

- o **Lists:** Break information into digestible points.

  '3 tips to boost your productivity: 1) Time blocking. 2) Limit distractions. 3) Take breaks.'
- o **Infographics:** Visual representations of complex topics.

  'Understanding blockchain in five steps [visual chart].'
- o **Myth-busting hooks: Address common beliefs.**

  'Think detox drinks cleanse your liver? Think again!'
- o **Carousel posts:** Swipe-able, step-by-step explanations.

Examples:

- o **Health:** 'Myth: Carbs are bad for you. Truth: Whole grains and complex carbs are essential for energy and health.'
- o **Finance:** 'Top 3 investments to start before 30: 1) Index funds. 2) Emergency fund. 3) Retirement accounts.'
- o **Tech:** 'Why AI won't replace your job (but will make it easier).'

3.5.4 Entertaining

Purpose: Capture attention with humour, relatable content, or trends.

Tactics:

- o **Memes**: Relatable visuals paired with witty text.

  'When your to-do list stares at you like… #MondayMood.'

- o **Trending sounds/challenges**: Use viral audio or participate in challenges.

  'That one co-worker who always eats your snacks… (with trending audio).'

- o **Stories**: Share quirky or light-hearted moments.

  'True story: A cat just walked into our office meeting and stayed for the whole thing.'

Examples:

- o **Retail:** 'When you realize you left your wallet at home AFTER reaching the checkout line. #RetailLife'

- o **Education:** 'That moment when the teacher says "group project" and you make eye contact with your bestie.'

- o **Tech:** 'AI is great until it starts suggesting baby names and you're single.'

3.5.5 Storytelling + Community Building

Purpose: Share personal or brand experiences to connect emotionally.

Tactics:

- o **Hooks:** 'I never thought this would happen...'

- o **Before/after posts**: Highlight transformations or milestones.

'3 years ago, we had a dream. Today, we're a community 100,000 strong!'

- o **Testimonials**: Feature user stories to build credibility.

  'Meet Rashmi, a busy mom who transformed her life using our meal planner.'

- o **Branded hashtags**: Encourage community involvement.

  '#MyFitnessJourney with @OurBrand.'

Examples:

- o **Health:** 'Raj lost 30 lbs in 6 months with our programme. Here's how he did it!'

- o **Education:** 'From struggling with math to acing calculus— read Abhishek's story of determination.'

- o **Retail:** 'When our first order shipped, we had no idea how far we'd come. Thank you for 5 amazing years!'

3.5.6 Interactive Content

Purpose: Boost engagement through audience participation.

Tactics:

- o **Polls**: Simple and fun decision-making.

  'Coffee or tea? Comment your choice!'

- o **Contests**: Offer prizes for engagement.

  'Caption this photo for a chance to win a Rs 500 gift card!'

- o **Quizzes**: Personalized or fun content.

  'Which productivity tool matches your personality? Take our 1-minute quiz!'

- o **User challenges**: Encourage audience actions.

  '30-day gratitude challenge: Share one thing you're grateful for each day and tag us!'

Examples:

- o **Fitness:** 'What's your favourite workout? Vote below: 🏃 Cardio 🏋 Strength 🧘 Yoga.'
- o **Tech:** 'Which feature would you love next in our app? Vote now!'
- o **Fashion:** 'Show us your favourite summer outfit using #MyStyleToday for a chance to be featured.'

3.5.7 Promotional + Testimonials

Purpose: Showcase products/services and build trust with social proof.

Tactics:

- o **Hard-sell posts**: Focus on urgency and exclusivity.

  'Hurry! 50% off ends tonight at midnight! ⌛'
- o **Soft-sell posts**: Focus on benefits.

  'Transform your mornings with our time-saving planner. ✿'
- o **User testimonials**: Highlight real results.

  '"This app changed my life!" – @HappyUser.'
- o **Behind-the-scenes**: Show product creation or unboxing.

Examples:

- o **Retail:** 'Limited-time offer: Get our signature handbag for $99 (originally $199). Don't miss out!'
- o **Tech:** 'See why 10,000+ users love our AI-powered writing tool. Start your free trial today!'
- o **Health:** 'Feeling tired all day? Try our energy-boosting smoothies, loved by 1,000+ customers.'

3.5.8 Activism, Awareness, Social Impact

Purpose: Showcase your brand's values and contributions.

Tactics:

- o **Calls to action**: Encourage community participation.

  'Join us in planting 1,000 trees this Earth Day! 🌱'

- o **Updates**: Share impact statistics.

  'Thanks to you, we donated Rs 100,000 to support education programmes.'

- o **Awareness posts**: Leverage impactful visuals or videos.

  '1 in 3 people don't have access to clean water. Let's change that. 💧'

Examples:

- o **Health:** 'For every bottle purchased, we'll donate one to a child in need.'

- o **Tech:** 'Proud to support women in STEM. Check out our latest scholarship recipients.'

- o **Education:** 'We're funding schools in underserved areas—here's the story of one village we helped.'

4

Search Engine Optimization: A Marathon, Not a Sprint

AFTER TAKING THE FIRST BIG STEP INTO DIGITAL marketing—creating your business website—you are full of excitement, ready to watch the orders roll in. But days go by, and the silence is deafening. You start refreshing your analytics—zero visitors, zero clicks. It feels like shouting into a void.

Then someone says, 'You need SEO.' At first, you think, 'okay, I'll add some keywords; how hard can it be?' But the deeper you dive, the more it feels like trying to solve a puzzle with missing pieces. Should you focus on backlinks? Meta descriptions? Or stuffing more keywords in articles? Why is everyone talking about algorithms like they're a secret code only experts understand? Why is this a continuous process?

Let me simplify this game for you so that you are well-versed with the rules and can play a long-term game with your team. But before that, let us look into a real-time story.

Dinesh Prasad ran a small furniture store in Lucknow, creating stunning pieces that blended traditional designs with modern aesthetics. Despite having a website showcasing his work, he struggled to attract customers beyond his local area.

After implementing a targeted SEO strategy focused on long-tail keywords like 'handcrafted Maharajganj modern furniture' and optimizing for local searches, Dinesh saw a roughly 320 per cent increase in organic traffic within six months. This led to a surge in inquiries from across India, and even international customers. It transformed his small workshop into a thriving business with thousands of customers across the globe.

This is the power of SEO. And there are countless examples of how SEO helps businesses drive sales—and exponential growth—through increased organic search visibility.

What About You?

Just because you have a website doesn't mean it'll get the traction you're hoping for. Without actively working behind the scenes, your site won't achieve its full potential:

- You won't get the traffic you need.
- You'll struggle to generate quality leads.
- Your online sales will remain stagnant.

I've seen this scenario play out countless times.

- For the local jeweller who made great products but couldn't attract customers online.
- For the real estate agent with a nice website that no one visited.
- For the family-owned bakery whose delicious foods were invisible to online searchers.
- For the new tech start-up which, despite its innovative product, didn't show up in relevant searches.

The list is endless.

These businesses made the same mistake: they thought just having a website was enough. But that's like opening a store in the middle of a desert and expecting customers to stumble upon it.

Do you relate to this kind of situation? Is your business also not driving enough traffic from search engines, because your website is not showing up on top of the search results for the keywords relevant to your business?

So, what's the point of even having a website?

Here's the fact: your website is your online shop, and like a real shop, it needs visitors to do well. To grow your business, you need to bring people to your site. That can happen in one of these ways:

- Drive traffic from search engines like Google and Bing, or popular social media platforms like Facebook, Instagram, YouTube, etc.

- Use paid ads (on search, social media, or third-party platforms).

- Rely on direct traffic (which typically happens when your business has become a brand).

In this chapter, I'll focus on the most effective and affordable method: driving traffic via search engines. I'll show you how to use SEO to help your business appear when potential customers are looking for what you offer.

4.1 Understanding Search Engine Optimization

Search engine optimization involves improving your website's ranking to increase its visibility when people look for products or services related to your business on Google, Bing, and other search engines. The better your SEO, the higher your website appears in search results, making it more likely for potential customers to find you.

Let's say you run a bakery in Bengaluru. When someone searches 'best French pastries in Bangalore', you want your website to show up on the first page of results. *Why?* Because most people don't look beyond the first page.

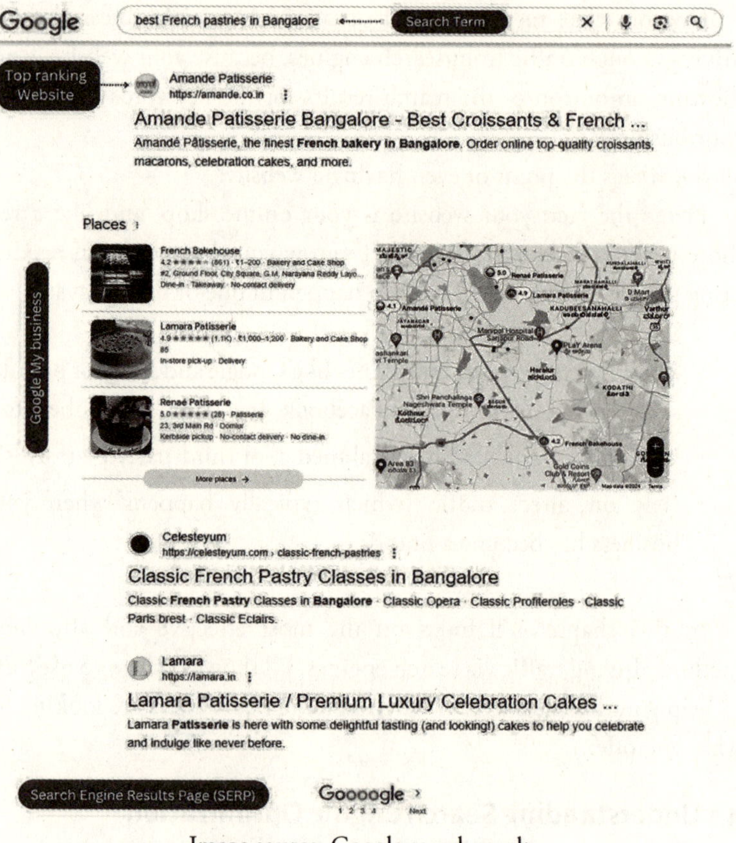

Image source: Google search results

SEO helps you:

- Drive free, targeted traffic to your site.
- Build credibility and trust with potential clients.
- Stay competitive in your market.

In general, it involves implementing a range of steps and tactics:

- Optimizing the website's content and structure.
- Creating relevant content with the right keywords relevant to one's product/services.
- Building quality links from other websites, in a process known as backlinking (the practice of earning links from other websites to your own, with the goal of improving search engine rankings and increasing website traffic).
- Ensuring site loads quickly and works well on mobile and other devices.

By implementing these SEO steps and tactics, the bakery could increase its online visibility, get more orders, and ultimately grow their business—all without paying a single penny to Google or any third party.

Understanding Its Three Components

Search engine optimization has three main parts: on-page, off-page, and technical. Think of them as three pillars holding up your website's visibility. Each plays a unique role in boosting your site's rankings and attracting more relevant visitors.

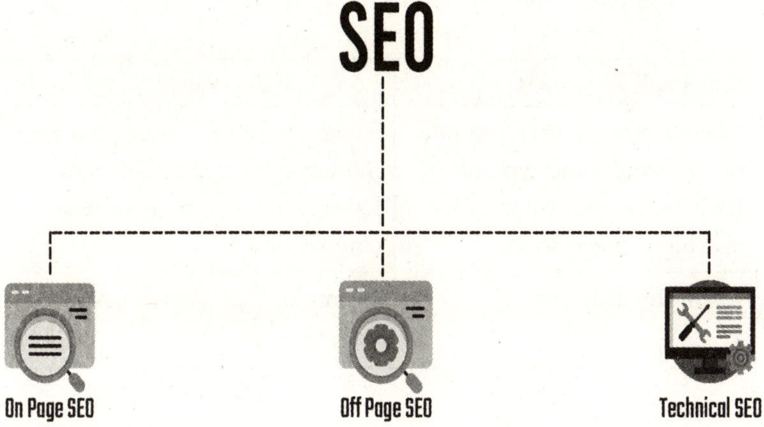

4.2 On-Page SEO

On-page SEO helps individual web pages rank higher in search engines, and attract relevant traffic. It broadly involves adjusting both the content and HTML source code of a page.

Here's what comes under on-page SEO:

Image source: Author's illustration

4.2.1 Keyword Research

Keyword research helps you find the words and phrases people use when searching for information related to your business or topic. It involves identifying terms relevant to your website's content, and analysing their search volume and competition.

You'll encounter different types of keywords.

Short-tail keywords	Long-tail keywords
These are brief, often just one or two words, and typically have high search volumes but also high competition.	These are longer phrases that are more specific and usually have lower search volumes but less competition.
Example: 'Buy pastries'	**Example**: 'Buy French pastries in Bangalore'

Once you've identified your keywords, you'll use them naturally throughout your webpage's content. This includes placing them in titles, headings, and body text.

4.2.2 Website Content

A search engine's algorithm scans through your website content to understand what is it about, and to determine its relevance to the user's queries. Good content has two important purposes. First, it helps search engines categorize and rank your site. Second, it provides value to your visitors, encouraging them to stay on your site longer, and eventually take desired actions.

The quality of your content affects your SEO performance. Search engines favour websites with original, informative, and regularly updated content. They look for content that addresses user intent (the reason behind a search query).

4.2.3 Title Tags and Meta Descriptions

Title tags and meta descriptions are HTML elements that provide concise summaries of your webpage's content. They appear in search engine results pages (SERPs) and influence how users decide whether to click on your page.

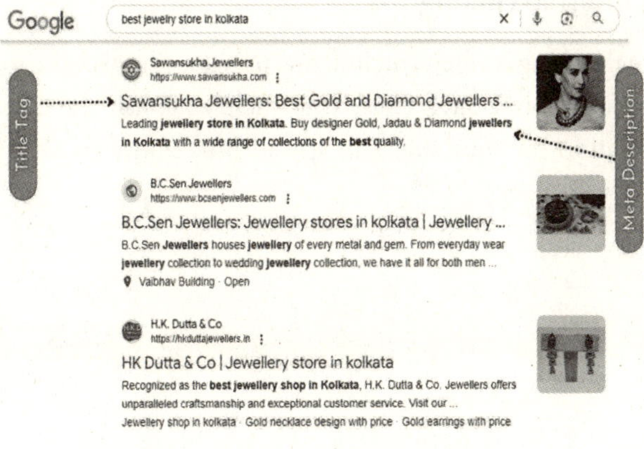

Image source: Google search results

Your title tag is the main text that describes your page. It appears as a clickable headline in search engine results. Meta descriptions are short summaries of your page's content. While they don't directly influence rankings, they can affect whether users choose to visit your page.

4.2.4 URL Structure

Your URL structure is how your website's addresses are formatted. A well-structured URL is easy for both humans and search engines to read and understand. It typically includes words that describe your page's content, often incorporating relevant keywords.

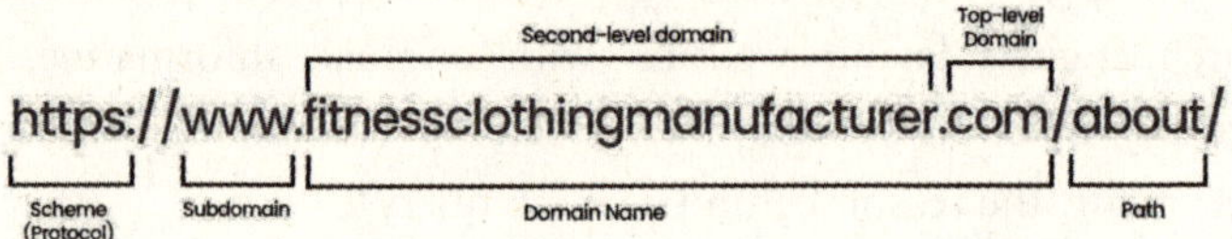

Clear URL structures help your users understand what a page is about before they click on it. They also provide search engines with additional context about your page's content, and how it fits into your overall website structure.

4.2.5 Internal Linking

Internal linking is when you link one page on your website to another page on the same site. These links help establish the hierarchy of information on your site, and spread link equity (ranking power) among your pages.

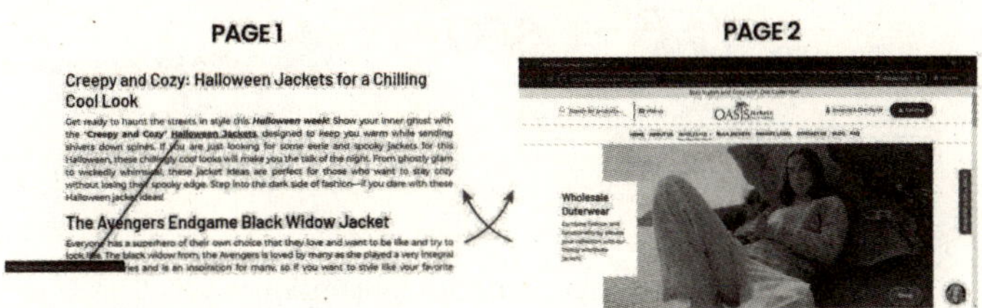

A good internal linking structure helps users navigate your website more easily, finding related content that might interest them. It also helps search engines understand the relationship between different pages and sections of your website.

4.2.6 Image Optimization

Optimizing images on your website includes adding descriptive file names and alternate (alt) text, which help search engines understand what the images depict. Alt text also improves accessibility for users who rely on screen readers.

When you optimize your images, it helps in overall optimization of your website. This precisely ensures visual quality with file size to enable fast page loading time.

4.3 Off-Page SEO

Off-page SEO focuses on improving your website's authority and credibility through actions taken outside of your own website.

Here's what falls under off-page SEO:

Image source: Author's illustration

4.3.1 Creating Keyword-Targeted Content

Producing valuable, keyword-focused content enhances off-page SEO by attracting backlinks and brand mentions. Content like blogs, videos, or infographics optimized for audience interests and search intent encourages sharing and citation by authoritative sites, boosting credibility and online visibility. Prioritize topics that solve problems or align with industry trends.

4.3.2 Submission to Authoritative and Relevant Sites

Search engines value links from credible and relevant websites. Think of it like this—if a budding cricketer gets endorsed by a respected figure like Sourav Ganguly, they'll gain recognition. Similarly, if ESPNCricinfo highlights their talent, it reinforces credibility.

For your site, authoritative and relevant backlinks act as these endorsements, boosting your search rankings.

4.3.3 Generating High-Quality Backlinks

Backlinks signal to search engines that your content is valuable. Focus on earning links from reputable and relevant websites by:

- Creating share-worthy content.
- Collaborating with other sites.

o   Being featured in news articles.

BACK LINKING

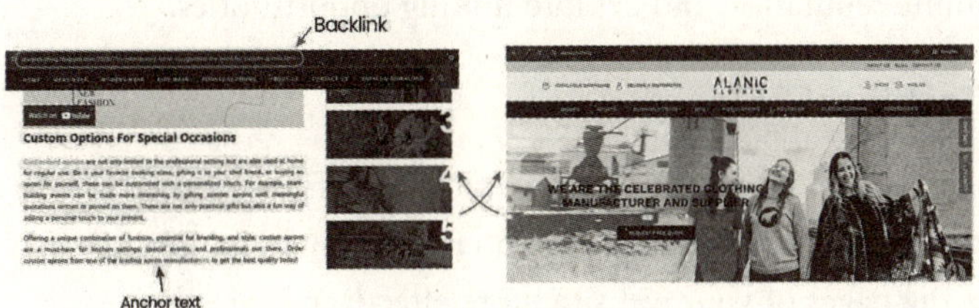

4.3.4 Guest Blogging

Writing for other industry relevant websites builds backlinks, enhances visibility, and establishes authority. Ensure the content aligns with the host site's audience and provides value. Backlinks are often included in the article or author bio.

4.3.5 Social Media Presence

While social media signals don't directly influence rankings, they increase visibility and drive traffic. Choose platforms where your audience is most active and engage meaningfully to amplify content sharing and potential backlinks.

4.3.6. Online Reviews and Ratings

Positive reviews on platforms like Google Business Profile and Yelp improve local SEO and build trust. Encourage satisfied customers to leave reviews and respond thoughtfully to all feedback, positive or negative. The quantity, quality, and recency of reviews influence their SEO impact.

4.3.7 Brand Mentions

Unlinked brand mentions in articles, blogs, or social media indicate credibility to search engines. Monitor mentions to understand your online reputation and explore linking opportunities.

4.4 Technical SEO

This focuses on improving the technical aspects of your website to help search engines crawl better ,i.e. to enable search engines to scan and index the pages of your website more effectively.

Here's what comes under it:

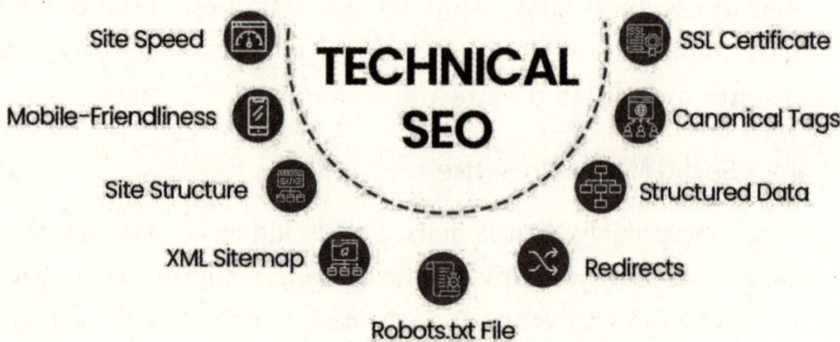

Image source: Author's illustration

4.4.1 Site Speed

This refers to how quickly your web pages load. Faster sites keep visitors engaged and reduce bounce rates. Search engines also prioritize faster sites in rankings. Factors like hosting, image size, file size, and site coding influence speed. Tools like Google PageSpeed Insights can identify issues and offer solutions.

4.4.2 Mobile-Friendliness

Mobile-friendliness ensures your site works seamlessly on smartphones and tablets. With more users browsing on mobile, search engines rank mobile-friendly sites higher. A mobile-friendly site adjusts layouts for smaller screens, making content readable without zooming or horizontal scrolling.

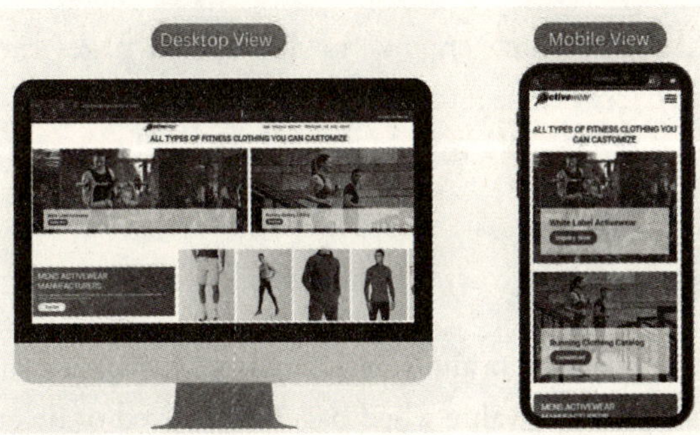

4.4.3 Site Structure

This is how your pages are organized and linked. A clear structure—with a logical hierarchy of categories and subcategories—helps users and search engines navigate your site. Internal links and clean URLs reflect a good site structure.

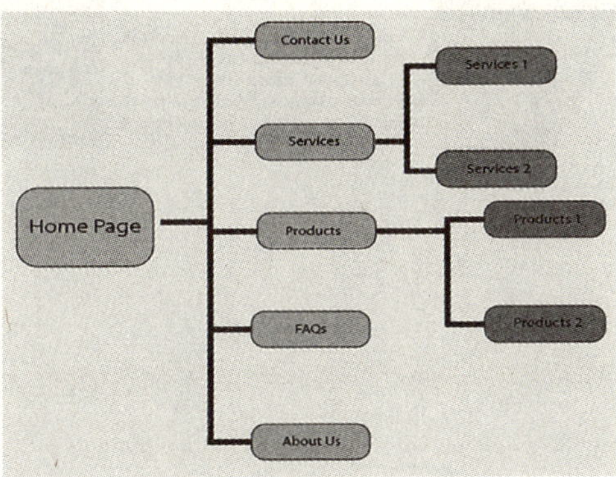

Image source: Author's illustration

4.4.4 XML Sitemap

An XML sitemap lists all important pages on your site, acting as a roadmap for search engines. It's especially useful for large or complex sites, helping search engines discover and index your content efficiently.

4.4.5 Robots.txt File

This file tells search engine crawlers which pages they should or shouldn't access. Use it to block non-essential or duplicate pages, but configure it carefully to avoid unintentionally blocking important content.

4.4.6 Redirects

Redirects guide users and search engines from one URL to another, maintaining SEO value when pages are moved or deleted. Use 301 redirects for permanent changes and 302 redirects for temporary ones to preserve link equity and ensure a smooth experience.

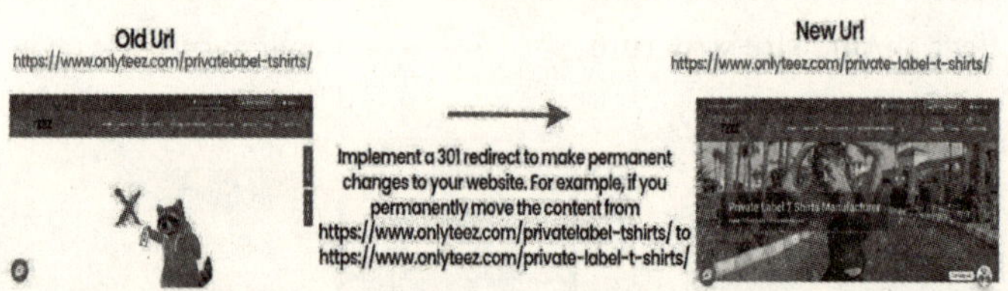

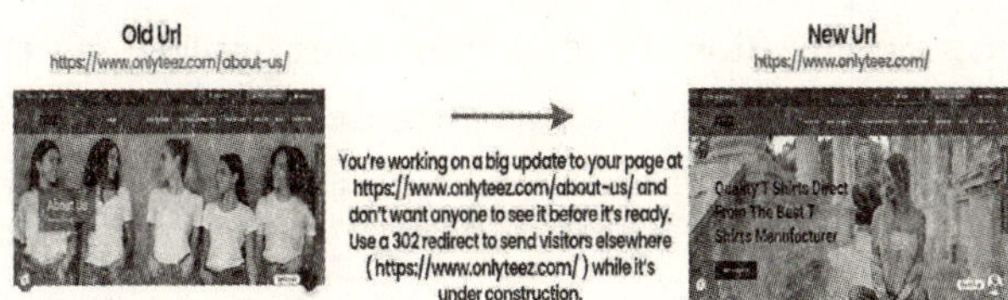

4.4.7 Structured Data

Structured data uses a standardized format to help search engines understand your content. It enables rich results (e.g., recipes, reviews, events) on search engine result pages, improving click-through rates which is the number of clicks your Ad receives divided by the number of times (impressions) your Ad is shown

4.4.8 Canonical Tags

Canonical tags manage duplicate content by specifying the 'master' version of a page. This consolidates SEO value and ensures search engines rank the right URL, useful for product pages with sorting options.

4.4.9 SSL Certificate

An SSL certificate authenticates your website and enables secure, encrypted connections (HTTPS). It's crucial for sites handling sensitive information and is a ranking factor, as search engines prioritize secure sites.

4.5 The Five SEO Sprints: Working with a Structured Approach

Search engine optimization involves numerous moving parts. A structured approach helps you manage these elements effectively and achieve results. Enter SEO sprints.

What Are SEO Sprints?

These break down your SEO strategy into manageable, time-boxed cycles. You focus on specific tasks or goals during each sprint, typically lasting two to four weeks. This approach allows you to tackle SEO systematically, measure progress, and adapt quickly.

I've found sprints particularly effective for our clients. They provide clear direction and help maintain momentum. Instead of getting overwhelmed by the big picture, you're making steady progress on bite-sized tasks.

I've broken down implementing an SEO strategy into five sprints.

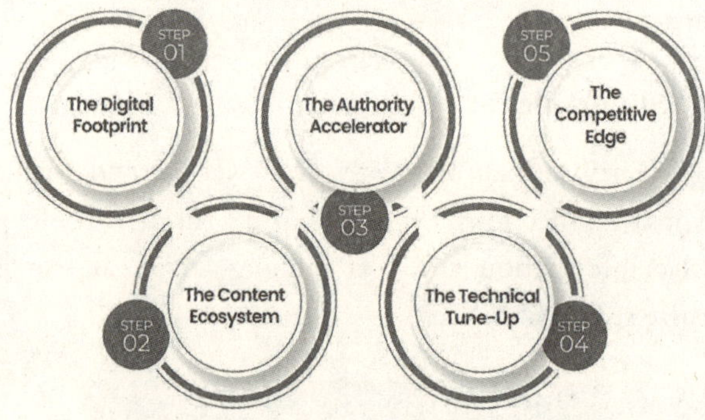

Image source: Author's illustration

Sprint 1: The Digital Footprint

Your digital footprint forms the foundation of your online presence. In this sprint, we'll focus on setting up and optimizing your core online assets. Here's what you need to do:

1. **Secure your domain name**: Choose a memorable, brand-relevant domain. I typically recommend '.com' for its universal recognition.

2. **Set up hosting**: Invest in reliable, fast hosting. Your site's performance depends on this, so don't cut corners.

3. **Install SSL certificate**: This encrypts data and gives you that 'HTTPS' in your URL. It's non-negotiable for security and SEO.

4. **Build your website**: Create a clean, professional site that represents your brand well. Remember, this is often your first impression on potential customers.

5. **Create essential pages**: About Us, Contact, Privacy Policy, Terms of Service—these build trust with users and search engines.

6. **Set up a blog or news section**: This lays the groundwork for your future content strategy.

7. **Optimize for mobile**: Ensure your site functions flawlessly on all devices. I've seen mobile optimization double conversion rates for some clients.

8. **Implement on-page SEO**: Optimize title tags, meta descriptions, headers, and content with relevant keywords. This helps search engines understand what your pages are about.

9. **Implement internal linking**: Connect your pages logically to spread link juice and guide users through your site.

10. **Optimize images**: Compress images and use descriptive file names and alt text. This simple step can improve page load times.

11. **Set up Google Analytics and Google Search Console**: These free tools provide insights into your website's performance and help you identify areas for improvement.

12. **Create your Google Business Profile**: This helps establish your online presence for local searches.

13. **Establish social media presence**: Choose platforms where your audience is most active. You don't need to be everywhere, but maintain a consistent brand image across the platforms you choose.

14. **Ensure NAP consistency**: Your name, address, and phone number should be consistent across all online platforms. This builds trust with both users and search engines.

Take your time with each of these steps. They form the foundation of your online presence, and getting them right sets you up for success in future sprints. I've seen businesses rush through this stage, only to struggle later, because their foundation wasn't solid.

Search engine optimization is a marathon, not a sprint. This first phase might seem like a lot of work without immediate results, but trust me, it's very important. Once you've completed these tasks, you'll have a strong digital footprint to build upon.

Sprint 2: The Content Ecosystem

In this sprint, we'll focus on building a robust content strategy. Content is the lifeblood of your SEO efforts; it's how you attract, engage, and convert your audience. Let's break down the key elements:

15. **Conduct keyword research**: Start by identifying the terms your target audience is searching for. Use tools like Google Keyword Planner, Semrush, or Ahrefs to find relevant keywords with good search volume and manageable competition.

16. **Create a content calendar**: Plan your content in advance. This helps maintain consistency and ensures you're covering all important topics in your niche.

17. **Develop pillar content**: These are comprehensive, authoritative pieces on core topics in your industry.

18. **Write blog posts**: Regular, high-quality blog posts keep your site fresh and give search engines more content to index. Aim for a mix of evergreen and timely content.

19. **Optimize existing content**: Don't neglect your old content, if you have any. Update and improve your existing pages to keep them relevant and valuable.

20. **Implement content clustering**: Group related content together to establish topic authority. This strategy has helped many of my clients improve their search rankings.

21. **Create diverse content types**: Don't limit yourself to just text. Incorporate images, videos, infographics, and interactive elements to engage different user preferences.

22. **Develop a link-building strategy**: Start planning how you'll acquire high-quality backlinks. This often involves creating link-worthy content.

23. **Implement internal linking**: Connect your blog posts logically. This helps users navigate your site and distributes page authority (see Sprint 3).

24. **Set up content tracking**: Use analytics to understand which content performs best and why. This informs your future content strategy.

25. **Optimize for featured snippets**: Structure your content to increase your chances of appearing in Google's featured snippets. This can significantly boost visibility.

Quality trumps quantity. It's better to publish one exceptional piece of content than several mediocre ones. Focus on creating value for your audience, and the SEO benefits will follow. In my experience, businesses that invest time in building a solid content ecosystem see long-term SEO success. It's not just about ranking; it's about establishing your brand as an authority in your field.

In the next sprint, we'll look at how to amplify your content and build authority through strategic partnerships and outreach.

Sprint 3: The Authority Accelerator

Authority in SEO determines how much search engines trust your site. This sprint focuses on building that trust through strategic link-building and brand promotion.

Think of it as your site's reputation. Just like in real life, your online authority grows when respected sources vouch for you. We'll work on getting high-quality websites to link to yours, effectively telling Google that your content is valuable and trustworthy.

Let's break down the key elements of this sprint:

26. **Identify link-building opportunities**: Research websites in your industry that might link to your content. Look for relevant blogs, news sites, and industry publications.

27. **Create link-worthy content**: Develop high-quality, unique content that others will want to link to. This could be original research, comprehensive guides, or innovative tools.

28. **Guest posting**: Reach out to reputable sites in your niche and offer to contribute guest posts. This builds your authority and often includes a link back to your site.

29. **Broken link building**: Find broken links on other sites and offer your content as a replacement. It's a win-win—you get a backlink, and they fix a broken link on their site.

30. **Digital PR**: Develop newsworthy content and reach out to journalists and bloggers. Getting mentioned in the press can significantly boost your authority.

31. **Participate in industry forums and discussions**: Share your expertise on platforms like Quora or industry-specific forums. While these links are often nofollow links i.e an attribute of a hyperlink that instructs search engines not to consider the link for search engine ranking calculations, however they still contribute to your overall online presence.

32. **Grow on social media**: While social signals aren't direct ranking factors, a strong social media presence can lead to more visibility and natural backlinks.

33. **Monitor brand mentions**: Set up alerts for your brand name and key products. When you're mentioned without a link, reach out and ask if they'd be willing to add one.

Authority building is a long-term game. It's not about quick wins, but about consistently proving your expertise and value. I always tell my clients to focus on creating genuinely helpful, shareable content and building real relationships in their industry.

In the next sprint, we'll dive into the technical aspects of SEO, ensuring your site is optimized from the ground up.

Sprint 4: The Technical Tune-Up

Technical SEO ensures search engines can efficiently crawl, understand, and index your content. While content and links often get the spotlight, poor technical SEO can undermine all your other efforts. Think of it as tuning a car's engine—it's not visible, but it's crucial for peak performance.

In this sprint, we'll focus on optimizing the nuts and bolts of your website. Here's what needs to be taken care of:

34. **Site-speed optimization**: Improve your site's loading speed. Compress images, minimize code, and leverage browser caching.

35. **Mobile responsiveness**: Ensure your site works flawlessly on all devices. With mobile-first indexing, this is non-negotiable.

36. **URL structure**: Create clean, descriptive URLs that both users and search engines can easily understand.

37. **XML sitemap**: Generate and submit an XML sitemap to help search engines discover and index all your important pages.

38. **Robots.txt**: Use this file to guide search engines on which parts of your site to crawl and which to ignore.

39. **Schema markup**: Implement structured data to help search engines understand your content better. This can lead to rich snippets in search results.

40. **HTTPS implementation**: If you haven't already, secure your site with SSL. It's now a ranking factor.

41. **Fix broken links and redirects**: Identify and fix any 404 errors and implement proper 301 redirects where necessary.

42. **Improve site architecture**: Ensure your site has a logical structure that's easy for users as well as search engines to navigate.

43. **Optimize for Core Web Vitals**: Focus on improving the largest contentful paint (LCP), a core web vital metric that measures how quickly the main content of a web page loads. 2.5 seconds or less for at least 75% of page visits is considered to be a good LCP. First Input Delay and Cumulative Layout

Shift are two other important vital metrics to consider in this regard. These metrics measure user experience, and contribute to the ranking factors.

Technical SEO might not be as visible as content creation or link building, but it's equally important. While implementing technical SEO is often quicker than building a content strategy, it can be challenging. You'll likely need to collaborate with technical SEO specialists and developers to implement these changes correctly.

In our final sprint, we'll look at how to stay ahead of the competition and adapt to the ever-changing SEO market.

Sprint 5: The Competitive Edge

Search engine optimization is dynamic, requiring constant adaptation and improvement. In this final sprint, we'll focus on advanced SEO tactics to stay ahead of your competitors.

This sprint is about pushing boundaries and exploring cutting-edge techniques. It's where you'll differentiate yourself from competitors. Here's what you need to do:

44. **Conduct competitive analysis**: Use tools like Semrush or Ahrefs to analyse your competitors' SEO strategies. Identify gaps in their approach that you can exploit. Look at their backlink profiles, content strategies, and keyword rankings. Pay attention to their top-performing pages and identify topics they're missing.

45. **Implement semantic SEO**: Go beyond keywords. Focus on topics and user intent. Use tools like Google's Natural Language API to understand how machines interpret your content. Create comprehensive topic clusters that cover all aspects of a subject. This helps establish topical authority and improves rankings for a wide range of related queries.

46. **Optimize for voice search**: Structure your content to answer specific questions. Use conversational language and focus on long-tail keywords. Create FAQ pages that directly address common voice queries in your niche. Optimize for featured snippets, as these are often used for voice search results.

47. **Leverage AI for content strategy**: Use AI tools to analyse search trends, generate topic ideas, and optimize headlines. Artificial Intelligence can help identify content gaps in your niche and predict which topics might gain traction. Tools like MarketMuse or Frase can provide AI-driven content briefs, helping you cover topics comprehensively. Use these insights to guide your human writers, ensuring your content meets user intent and covers topics thoroughly.

48. **Implement advanced schema markup**: Go beyond basic schema. Use Article, FAQ, How-to, and other advanced schemas to enhance your search appearance. Implement Review and Product schemas for e-commerce sites. Use Event schema for time-sensitive content. Regularly check Google's Search Gallery for new schema types you can leverage.

49. **Use programmatic SEO**: For large sites, use data and automation to create thousands of optimized pages. This works well for e-commerce and directory style sites. Implement dynamic title tags and meta descriptions based on user search queries and product attributes. Use APIs to automatically update content with real-time data.

50. **Implement international SEO**: If targeting global markets, use hreflang tags which specify language and regional targeting of a webpage. Consider creating separate sites for different markets with ccTLDs or subdirectories. Implement geo-targeting in Google Search Console.

These advanced tactics often require specialized skills. It's best to work with developers or hire SEO specialists.

The key to maintaining a competitive edge is staying informed about emerging trends and being willing to experiment. Search engine optimization rewards those who are proactive, not reactive. Your ability to quickly adapt to changes in the search market will be your greatest competitive advantage.

4.6 How to Complete These Sprints?

Implementing these sprints requires careful planning and coordination. Start by setting realistic deadlines for each sprint. Depending on your resources and the complexity of your website, each sprint might take two to four weeks. Be flexible, but try to maintain momentum.

Assemble your team. You'll likely need a mix of skills:

- Content writers
- Web developers
- SEO specialists
- Data analysts

If you don't have all these skills in-house, consider partnering with an SEO agency. Next:

- **Create a detailed project plan**: Break down each sprint into specific tasks, assign responsibilities, and set milestones. Use project management tools like Trello or Asana to keep everyone on track.
- **Establish regular check-ins**: Weekly team meetings can help address challenges, share progress, and adjust strategies as needed. These meetings keep everyone aligned and accountable.
- **Implement a system for tracking progress**. Use tools like Google Analytics and Google Search Console to monitor key metrics. Create dashboards that show improvements in rankings, traffic, and conversions.

- **Don't forget to document everything**. Create standard operating procedures (SOPs) for recurring tasks. This ensures consistency and makes it easier to train new team members.

In the end, be prepared to iterate; SEO is not a one-time effort. As you complete each sprint, you may identify new opportunities or challenges. Be ready to adjust your plan accordingly.

4.7 Local SEO or Google Business Profile (GBP)

Local SEO or GBP targets potential customers in your specific area. It focuses on geographic relevance and local search intent, helping your business appear when nearby customers need your products or services.

Picture this: A customer searches for 'best pizza near me' at 8 p.m. on a Saturday. If you're a local restaurant without proper local SEO, you're invisible to this potential customer. Local SEO ensures you show up when it matters most.

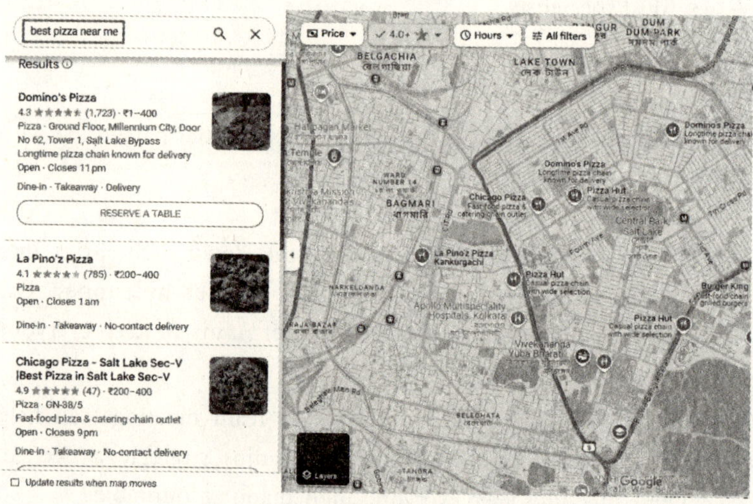

Image source: Google search results

Google Business Profile

Your Google Business Profile is the cornerstone of local SEO. It's what appears when people search for your business or related services in your area.

You need to set up this profile.

- Visit google.com/business and click 'Manage now'.
- Enter your business name and address.
- Choose your business category.
- Add your phone number and website.
- Verify your listing.

Optimizing Your Google Business Profile

Simply having a profile isn't enough. You need to optimize it to rank higher in local searches and Google Maps. You'll be able to do it from your dashboard.

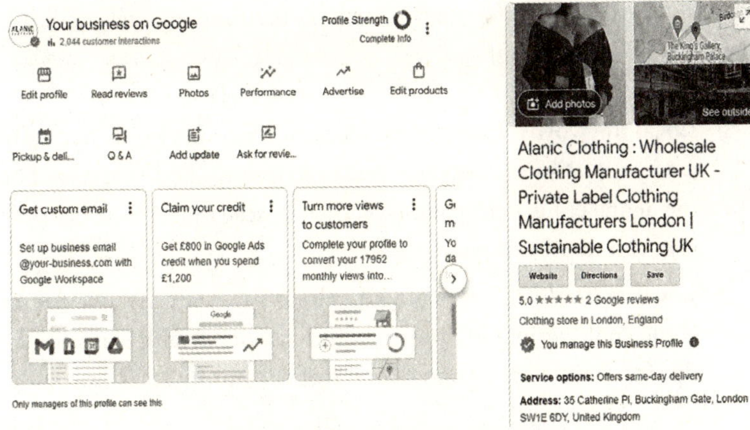

Image source: Google search results

Here's how to optimize your GBP, taking a dental clinic for example:

- **Complete every section**: Fill in all details like hours, services, and descriptions (e.g., list dental specialties and unique offerings).

- **Use high-quality photos**: Showcase your clinic's interior, staff, and equipment to attract and reassure patients.

- **Manage reviews**: Encourage reviews and respond professionally to all feedback.

- **Post regular updates**: Share offers or events to keep your profile active (e.g., 'free dental check-up this Sunday!').

- **Use attributes**: Highlight features like 'emergency dental care' to stand out.

- **Maintain NAP consistency**: Ensure your name, address, and phone match across platforms for better rankings.

4.8 Beyond Google Business Profile

While your Google Business Profile is important, it's not the only aspect of local SEO. You need to stick to the fundamentals of SEO, but with the local flavour.

- **Local keywords**: Incorporate location-based keywords naturally into your website content, meta descriptions, and title tags. For the dental clinic example used earlier, instead of just 'best dentist', use 'best dentist in [your city]'.

- **Local content**: Create content relevant to your area. A dental clinic could write blog posts about local oral health statistics, or tips for maintaining good dental hygiene during festivals.

- **Local link building**: Earn backlinks from other local businesses or organizations. Partner with local schools for dental awareness programmes or participate in community health events to build these connections.

- **Mobile optimization**: Many local searches take place on mobile devices. Ensure your website is mobile-friendly for the best user experience.

- **Local schema markup**: Use structured data to tell search engines about your local business information, like address and opening hours.

Local SEO helps you connect with the customers in your neighbourhood. Do it right, and you'll be the first business they see when they need what you offer. Whether you're a restaurant, a boutique, or a dental office, local SEO can put you on the map—literally and figuratively.

4.9 Impact of AI on SEO

Search engine optimization has evolved dramatically over the past two decades. In the early 2000s, it revolved around keyword stuffing and link quantity. Today, it focuses on user experience, content quality, and technical performance.

AI in Search Results

Artificial Intelligence is transforming how search engines work, and how users interact with results. A prime example is Google's Search Generative Experience (SGE), which displays AI-generated summaries at the top of search results, often reducing the need to click through to websites.

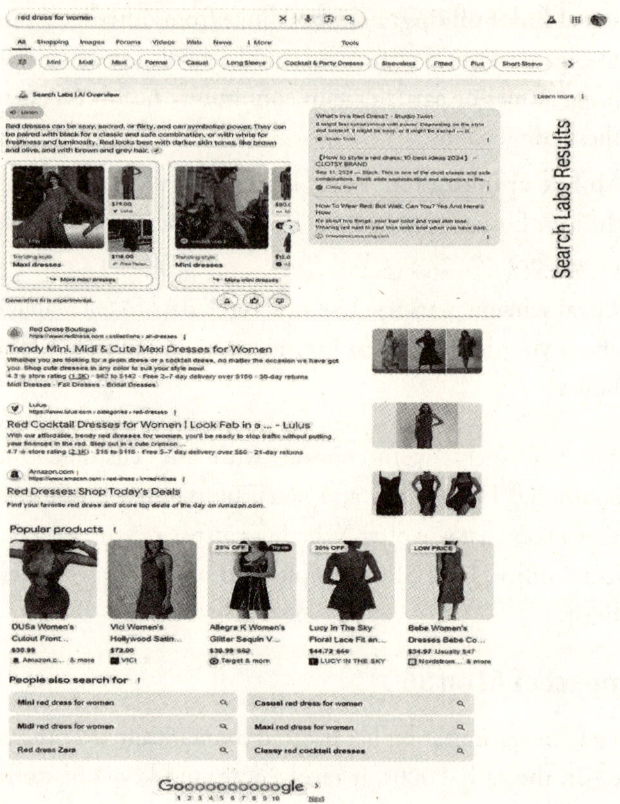

Image source: Google search results

This shift has impacted click-through rates, as traditional organic listings are pushed further down. To adapt, prioritize structured data, concise content, and directly answering user queries. Balancing optimization for traditional search results as well as AI-driven summaries is now essential. It's no longer just about ranking but becoming the source that AI references.

Search engine optimization is a long-term investment, requiring consistent effort and patience. Each step builds a stronger foundation for your brand. While SEO establishes your base, the next chapter explores Google and Meta ads—a faster way to amplify your reach and complement your SEO efforts.

4.10 Getting Started

Search engine optimization drives visibility and growth for Indian businesses across sectors. Myntra's category optimized pages and Swiggy's location-based SEO showcase its impact in e-commerce and food delivery. Even B2B companies like Zoho leverage SEO to compete globally.

To implement SEO effectively:

- Assess your current online presence.
- Define clear, measurable goals.
- Create custom sprints based on your priorities.
- Assign tasks to team members with relevant skills.
- Set realistic timelines for each sprint.
- Monitor progress and adjust strategies as needed.

5

Leveraging Advertising Powerhouses: Google and Meta Ads

'THE MORE YOU INVEST, THE MORE YOU EARN' IS A mantra often talked about when it comes to Google and Meta ads. But if not done right, the budget simply burns without much return.

Running ads on Google and Meta often feels like placing bets in a game where the house always wins. You're constantly tweaking audiences, creatives, and budgets. If it clicks, you can get your return on investment. But most of the time, you see impressions rise while conversions stay stagnant. Causing doubts to creep in: Am I doing this wrong? Is my product not getting enough searches? Is my business not good enough?

In my fifteen years of running campaigns, I've learned that success in paid ads often boils down to one thing—a solid framework. A smart one that follows a structured, proven approach. Many businesses rely on the R.A.C.E. framework to guide their online advertising efforts. It's a popular model that covers four key stages—Reach, Act, Convert, and Engage.

The T.R.A.C.E. framework, however, is a more accurate version to understand and evaluate. It involves Target, Reach, Act, Convert and Evaluate. Thus, it also focuses on evaluating what is working and what is not. I will be explaining the nitty gritty of this framework in detail as we move forward.

In this chapter, we'll understand the fundamentals of:

- ✓ Running ads online, and their benefits.
- ✓ How you can use them to drive sales.
- ✓ The R.A.C.E. and T.R.A.C.E. frameworks to help you start with Google and Meta ads.
- ✓ Various kinds of ads with practical examples.

'Modest Investments, Massive Returns'

Jignesh's small electronics repair shop in Surat was on the brink of closure. Local competition was fierce, and foot traffic had dwindled to almost nothing. In desperation, he turned to Google Ads.

With a modest budget of INR 15,000 per month, Jignesh targeted local searches for 'mobile repair near me' and 'laptop repair shop Surat'. The result? Within weeks, his shop was buzzing with new customers. His revenue doubled in just two months.

It's a similar story for a travel agency owner in Jaipur, who saw his business hit a wall after the COVID-19 pandemic. Despite his team's efforts to recover, foot traffic was low, and traditional advertising brought minimal returns.

Then, they turned to online ads. With carefully targeted Meta ads, they reached potential customers searching for post-pandemic travel deals. Within four months, their bookings tripled, and their revenue bounced back stronger than ever.

What About You?

Your business deserves to be seen. Right now, your perfect customers are out there, scrolling through Facebook or searching on Google. They're looking for what you offer, but can't find you.

Google and Meta ads—the two most popular ad platforms—change that. They put your business front and centre, where your customers are already looking.

From local shops to growing start-ups, businesses of all sizes use them to reach new customers and boost sales. And the best part? You can start small and scale up as you see results.

Let me quickly run down the basics before jumping to the interesting parts.

5.1 What Are Online Ads?

Online ads are paid messages that appear on platforms like search engines, websites, and social media. These ads can be a simple text message, an image or a video, but they all serve one purpose—to get your business in front of the right audience, or in other words, to connect you with your potential customer.

When you run an online ad, you pay the platform (like Google or Meta) to display your ad to people who match your target audience. This can be based on their searches, browsing habits, interests, or demographics. For example, if you're a local bakery, you can target people searching for 'best bakery near me' or show up in the feeds of users from a specified demographic who follow food-related pages on Facebook.

Google and Meta (which includes Facebook and Instagram) dominate the online advertising market. I'll be covering both in detail later in this chapter.

How Online Ads Work

- **You create an ad campaign**: Using the platform's tools, you design your ad and set parameters like budget and duration.

- **The platform displays your ad**: When someone searches on Google/YouTube or scrolls through Facebook/Instagram, the platform shows the ad to relevant users in real-time, based on search relevance, pre-set filters and your bid.

- **Users interact with your ad**: They might click, view, or take other actions.

- **You pay based on the interaction**: Depending on the selected pricing model, you're charged for these interactions.

- **You gain insights**: The platforms provide detailed analytics about your ad's performance.

How Payment Models Work in Online Ads

When you run online ads, you pay based on different models. The three main models are:

- **Cost per click (CPC)**: You pay each time someone clicks your ad. This is best for driving traffic to your website.

- **Cost per mille (CPM)**: You pay per thousand ad impressions. This is best for building brand awareness.

- **Cost per action (CPA)**: You pay when users complete a specific action (purchase, sign-up, more). This is best for driving conversions/sales.

How Online Ads Help

Online ads are a cost-effective way to drive results quickly, especially when budgets are tight. Here's how they benefit your business:

- **Target the right audience**: Reach people based on location, interests, age, or behaviours.

- **Quick visibility**: Ads provide instant exposure compared to slower methods like SEO.

- **Budget control**: Spend what you can afford, from INR 5,000 to INR 50,000, with full control.

- **Drive traffic**: Directly bring potential customers to your website or landing page.

- **Generate quality leads**: Targeted ads attract people already interested in your offerings.

- **Track performance**: Monitor ad impressions, clicks, and conversions easily.

- **Boost brand awareness**: Even unclicked ads build visibility and keep your brand top of mind.

5.2 The T.R.A.C.E. Framework

Back in 2018, I was working with a premium pet food brand. They were pouring money into ads, reaching tons of people, but sales were flat. We dug into the data and realized they were targeting all pet owners—but their product was perfect for a specific niche: health-conscious dog owners willing to pay a premium for organic food.

That's when we decided to adopt a more accurate framework: T.R.A.C.E. Here's how it works:

(i) Target

This is your foundation. Who exactly are you trying to reach? Say you're launching a high-end yoga mat. Instead of targeting 'yoga enthusiasts', we'd narrow it down to 'women, 28–45, living in metro cities, with disposable income, who attend yoga classes at least twice a week and follow wellness influencers on Instagram'.

See the difference? Now, we're not just reaching people—we're reaching the right people.

(ii) Reach

Now that we know who we're after, we can spread the message efficiently. For our yoga mat, we might use Instagram ads showcasing the mat in aspirational settings; Google ads targeting specific search terms like 'best premium yoga mat'; and partner with wellness YouTubers for sponsored content.

(iii) Act

This is where we encourage interaction. For example, we might create a landing page offering a free e-book on '10 Advanced Yoga Poses for a Stronger Core' in exchange for an email address. Now, we're not just shouting about our product—we're providing value and starting a relationship.

(iv) Convert

Turn that interest into sales. With our yoga mat, we could offer early bird purchasers a free online yoga class with a renowned instructor. It adds value and creates urgency.

(v) Evaluate

Most businesses skip this step, but it's absolutely crucial. We'd track sales, engagement rates, email open rates, which ad placements performed best, and more. Then, we'd use that data to refine our approach.

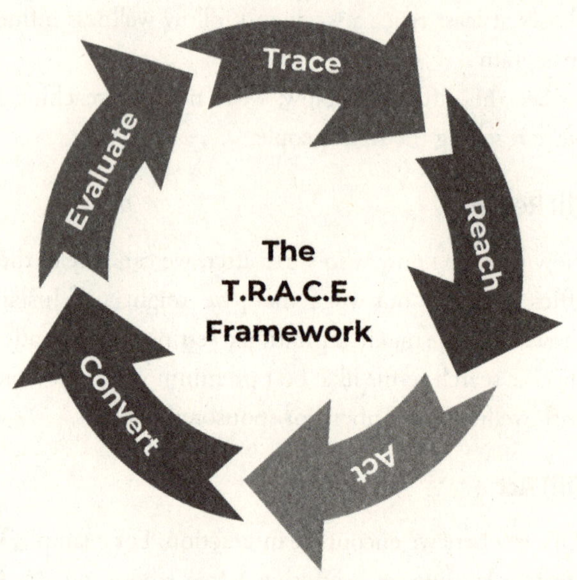

Image source: Author's illustration

The T.R.A.C.E. framework keeps your ad campaigns focused and efficient by targeting the right audience, saving time and money, and boosting conversions through clear, actionable steps. Its 'Evaluate' phase encourages continuous learning, ensuring your strategies improve over time.

Now, let's look individually at Google and Meta Ads, and how you can use the T.R.A.C.E. framework to create ad campaigns on Google, Facebook, and Instagram.

5.3 Google Ads

Google Ads is an online advertising platform that helps your business reach customers when they are searching for what you offer.

Imagine this: your perfect customer is already on Google, typing in words that match your product or service. Google Ads ensures your business appears right when they hit 'search'—essentially connecting you with users who are actively seeking what you provide.

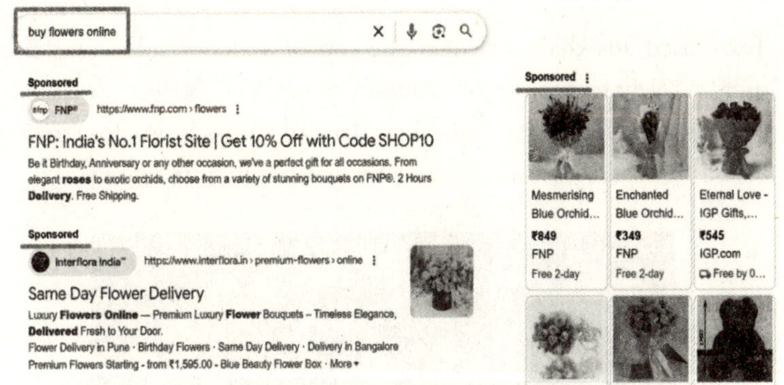

Image source: Google search results

How Google Ads Work

Google Ads work on a simple premise: you pay for visibility on Google's search results.

When users search for something relevant to your business, Google decides whether to show your ad based on a combination of factors, such as your bid amount, ad copy relevance, ad quality score etc.

The more precise and targeted your ad is, the better your chances of appearing in front of the right customers at the right time.

You have complete control over how you target customers, which means your ads can be as broad or as specific as you need them to be.

Importantly, you can track every click, view, and conversion, which allows you to fine-tune your strategy in real-time.

Google uses an ad auction to determine which ads are shown. This happens in milliseconds. The auction evaluates factors like the relevancy of your ad copy, the amount of your bid, and the quality of your landing page. Together, these factors form your Ad Rank, ultimately deciding if and where your ad will appear.

Types of Google Ads

Google Ads come in different forms to help you achieve your specific goals. Here are the main types:

5.3.1 Search Ads

Text-based ads that appear at the top of search results, targeting users actively searching for products or services. Perfect for driving immediate action. For example, a bakery running ads for 'freshly baked bread near me' saw increased foot traffic in two weeks.

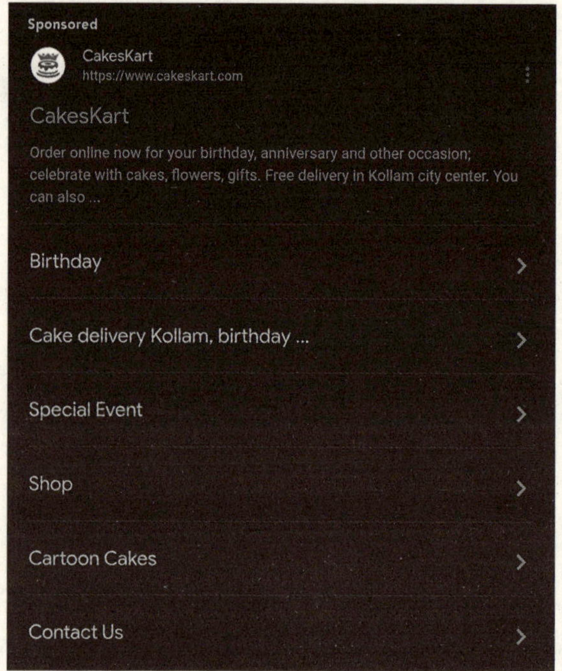

Source: Google search results

5.3.2 Display Ads

Image-based ads shown across Google's partner websites. Ideal for brand awareness and staying top-of-mind, even for users not actively searching. They can include rich media-like videos to attract viewers.

Image source: Cakeskart.com

5.3.3 Shopping Ads

Designed for e-commerce, these visually appealing ads display product images, prices, and store details directly in search results. They drive high-intent traffic to product pages.

Image source: Google search results

5.3.4 Video Ads

Runs on YouTube, the world's second-largest search engine. Great for storytelling, showcasing products, or sharing customer testimonials. For example, a yoga studio used video tutorials to boost enrolments and build a strong community.

Image source: YouTube ad

5.3.5 Local Services Ads or GBP Ads

Connects local businesses with nearby customers. Ideal for restaurants, healthcare services, retail stores, and service providers like electricians and travel agencies. Increases visibility for businesses with a physical presence.

5.3.6 App Ads

Focus on driving app downloads across Google Play, YouTube, and search. Google optimizes campaigns to find the best users, requiring minimal input.

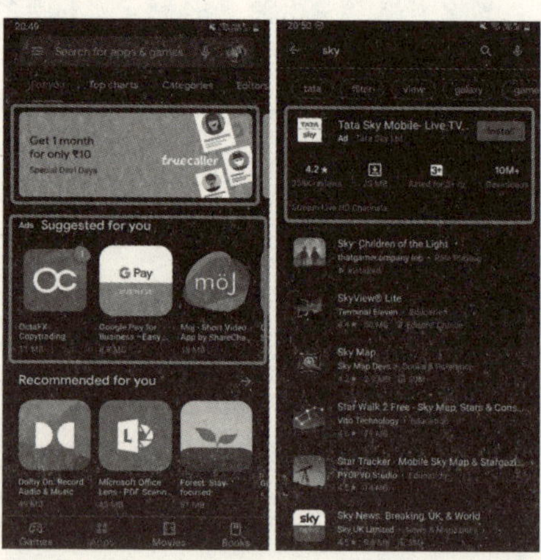

Image source: Mobile search options

Factors That Affect Google Ads

Google doesn't show ads randomly. As I mentioned earlier, there are various factors that affect ads' visibility and ranking.

- **Ad copy relevance**: Ads must match user searches. Relevant keywords and ad copy increase visibility.

- **Quality score**: Google rates your ad based on relevance, expected click-through rate, and landing page experience. Higher scores results in lower costs and better placement.

- **Bid amount**: Competitive bidding determines ad ranking. Balance your bid with a high quality score for cost-effective results.

- **Landing page experience**: Fast, mobile-friendly, and relevant landing pages improve performance. A poor experience lowers your ad's chances of appearing.

5.4 Creating a Google Ads Campaign Using T.R.A.C.E. Framework

Let's understand how you can use the T.R.A.C.E. framework to create a Google Ads campaign.

- **Target**: Identify a specific audience using Google's targeting tools (e.g., demographics, behaviour). For example, a local organic food service could target urban professionals aged 25–45 in specific delivery zones.

- **Reach**: Select ad types based on audience intent. Use Search Ads for high-intent queries like 'laptop repair near me', and Display Ads for passive awareness.

- **Act**: Align your landing page with your ad's promise. Simplify user actions, like booking a consultation or signing up, to improve conversions.

- **Convert**: Use urgency to drive action, like countdown timers or limited-time offers (e.g., '20% off for the next 50 customers!').

- **Evaluate**: Analyse metrics like CTR and ROAS to refine future campaigns. For example, shift focus to better-performing keywords or ad types.

5.5 Meta Ads

Meta Ads is the advertising platform used for both Facebook and Instagram. With billions of active users, Meta Ads can help your business connect with your ideal customers in highly personalized ways.

Imagine your perfect customer scrolling through their social feed and finding your business right there, ready to meet their needs. That's what Meta Ads make possible.

How Meta Ads Work

Meta Ads leverage Facebook and Instagram's user data to target the right audience for your products or services. These ads allow you to select platforms, target criteria, and budgets, ensuring your message reaches the right people.

One of the biggest strengths of Meta Ads is precision targeting. For example, my team helped a boutique in Mumbai target women aged 25–40 who were interested in sustainable fashion, leading to higher engagement and effective budget use.

With real-time performance tracking, you can fine-tune your campaign as it runs. Meta offers flexible pricing models like CPC, CPM, and CPA, allowing you to control spending while achieving your advertising goals.

Types of Meta Ads

Meta Ads come in different formats. This allows you to choose the one that best suits your campaign objectives. Here are the main types:

5.5.1 Image Ads

A single high-quality image can often make the right impact, especially when paired with engaging copy. This format works well for promoting products and events, or simply boosting brand awareness.

5.5.2 Video Ads

Videos are excellent for storytelling, showing product use, or creating an emotional connection.

My team once worked with a wellness centre in Bengaluru, and using short videos of yoga routines performed by local instructors, significantly boosted online registrations. People could see exactly what to expect, which helped them feel connected even before visiting.

5.5.3 Carousel Ads

These allow you to showcase multiple images or videos within a single ad that users can swipe through. This is perfect for displaying a variety of products or features.

5.5.4 Collection Ads

Designed to make shopping seamless, these ads combine a cover image or video with several product images. This makes it easy for users to discover products and make purchases right from their feeds.

5.5.5 Stories Ads

Stories are short-lived, immersive content appearing in their own separate section on Facebook and Instagram. Stories Ads create an immediate impact and are great for time-sensitive promotions.

5.5.6 Lead Ads

These ads are designed to collect user information directly on Facebook or Instagram. This is particularly useful for service-based businesses.

Imagine you're a mutual fund advisor; Lead Ads can help you gather information from prospects interested in a free consultation/ phone call/face-to-face meeting without them ever having to leave the platform.

5.6 Creating Meta Ads Campaign Using T.R.A.C.E. Framework

Now, let's apply the T.R.A.C.E. framework to create a Meta Ads campaign, specifically tailored for the Facebook and Instagram environment.

- **Target**: Use Meta's tools to define a precise audience based on interests, demographics, and behaviours. For example, for an eco-friendly decor campaign, target 'women aged 30–50, interested in sustainability, following home decor influencers'.

- **Reach**: Select ad formats and placements where your audience spends time, like Instagram Stories or Facebook feed. Use engaging content, such as videos showcasing transformations or product use, to capture attention.

- **Act**: Create clear CTAs like 'Shop Now' or 'Learn More'. For example, pair a video of handcrafted jewellery with a simple, actionable button to drive engagement.

- **Convert**: Use urgency to push action, such as '10% off if you book in the next 48 hours!' to turn interest into conversions.

- **Evaluate**: Leverage Meta analytics and tools like Meta Pixel to track key metrics (CTR, conversion rate). Use insights to refine and improve future campaigns.

5.7 How to Get Started: A Checklist

Getting started with Google and Meta Ads doesn't have to be overwhelming. Here's a quick checklist to help you kick off your campaigns efficiently and effectively:

- ✓ Define specific objectives and KPIs for your campaigns.
- ✓ Identify and segment your target audience.
- ✓ Perform keyword research for Google Ads, and select appropriate ad types for Meta.
- ✓ Set up tracking using Meta Pixel, Google Tag Manager, and Google Analytics.
- ✓ Create compelling ad copy and high-quality visuals.
- ✓ Choose your bidding model and allocate your budget.
- ✓ Launch the campaign with a small budget to gather insights.
- ✓ Monitor performance metrics and make adjustments.
- ✓ Continuously evaluate and refine your campaigns.

6

Story, Reels, Live, and More:
The Instagram Game

Most of the world wakes up to Instagram. Scrolling through the feed takes precedence over our daily chores. As a result, naturally, there is a frenzy among brands to dive in.

But in spite of investing loads of time, money, and energy into Instagram, founders and business owners are, more often than not, left wondering if they'll ever see a tangible ROI.

Are you too exhausted from pouring resources into Instagram ads, chasing trends, and staging perfect photoshoots, only to see mediocre results? Likes don't pay the bills, conversions do! Are you ready to play it like a pro?

If yes, I have developed a framework that will give you a 360-degree approach to get the maximum out of Instagram. It's called L.I.F.T., and it attempts to lift your overall game. I have discussed the framework in detail in the following pages.

Before I get to the details, I have a fundamental question to ask you. Please take a five-minute pause and answer.

What Do You Want to Do (or Solve) on Instagram?

Instagram offers endless possibilities, but the first step is to define your purpose. Here are some goals you might want to achieve:

- **Educate and provide value**: Establish your expertise by sharing insights or knowledge that helps your audience.

- **Generate leads and drive sales**: Attract new customers and create a seamless journey from discovery to purchase.

- **Build your company's brand**: Craft a narrative that resonates with your audience and sets your brand apart.

- **Establish your personal brand**: Build your reputation as an industry leader by sharing valuable and relatable content.

- **Improve customer service**: Make customer support more accessible and proactive.

- **Plan product launches or announcements**: Create impactful campaigns to drive engagement and excitement for new launches.

- **Expand your reach through collaborations**: Partner with influencers or businesses to grow your audience and credibility.

- **Promote events and drive attendance**: Boost participation in webinars, product demos, or industry events.

There's a range of professional or business goals you may have. Instagram, with its massive user base, is the platform to be on, no matter what you want to achieve.

But just existing on Instagram and passively posting pictures doesn't help. I've seen a fair share of fail stories of brands aimlessly posting content on the app—yielding no meaningful returns whatsoever.

You need a strategy. Why? Because while creating an image (visual, copy) is an art, you need science to make it work. I recommend the L.I.F.T. framework. Let me break it down for you.

6.1 The L.I.F.T. Framework

The L.I.F.T. framework is a comprehensive approach to Instagram marketing that focuses on four key pillars: Leverage, Inspire, Focus, and Track. This is a model we use for our clients. It helps businesses and individuals maximize their impact on the platform by

- using all available features optimally.
- creating compelling content.
- maintaining brand consistency.
- continuously improving based on data-driven insights.

Some marketing strategists on the internet insist on following a strict blueprint for Instagram growth, telling you that if you don't stick to their framework—whether it's using specific content types, posting schedules, or trends—you can't succeed.

But this approach often ignores the importance of aligning your content with your brand's true values, following rigid, one-size-fits-all strategies.

The L.I.F.T. framework works by providing a structured yet flexible methodology for Instagram success by working on the fundamentals. You can use it to adapt to the platform's evolution while staying true to its core objectives.

Let me explain each of these steps in detail for you to apply and understand the best way to use Instagram for your brand.

6.1.1 Leverage—the Features

Leverage, the first step in the L.I.F.T. framework, focuses on maximizing Instagram's features. This means understanding and using each feature purposefully to support your goals instead of going all cuckoo.

Stories, Reels, Live broadcasts, and other tools all serve different purposes. Knowing when and how to use each feature helps create a strong, diverse Instagram presence. Effective leveraging engages your audience across multiple touchpoints, increasing your impact on the platform.

a) Single-Image Posts

Single-image posts are static visuals shared on the main Instagram feed. They appear on followers' feeds and can be discovered via hashtags, location tags, and the Explore page.

Ideal for: Standalone visuals, announcements, product showcases, or concise brand messaging.

Example: Zomato's single image post on the company's birthday, highlighting everything in one go.

Image source: Moves of Marketing Instagram page, 2024[1]

b) Carousel

Carousel posts allow up to twenty images or videos in a single post, enabling extended storytelling within one upload. Each slide can have a different format, and carousels include captions, tags, and location info.

Ideal for: Step-by-step guides, showcasing multiple products, event highlights, or visual storytelling.

Example: An image from Apple's carousel post, highlighting the extraordinary quality of visuals from the iPhone 16 Pro.

Image source: Apple Instagram page, 2024[2]

c) Reels

Reels are short-form vertical videos lasting up to ninety seconds, designed for engaging and dynamic content. They feature creative tools like music, effects, and text overlays. Reels appear in the main feed, a dedicated Reels tab, and on the Explore page.

Ideal for: Quick tutorials, trends, showcasing products, or increasing discoverability via Reels' algorithm.

Image source: Aamir Wani (Kashmir Through My Lens)
Instagram page, 2024[3]

Example: Dynamic visual representation of a creator on Kashmir.

d) Direct Messages (DMs)

Instagram DMs allow private messaging with text, voice, photos, videos, and posts. Features include disappearing messages and custom chat colours.

Ideal for: Customer service, networking, private conversations, and building one-on-one relationships.

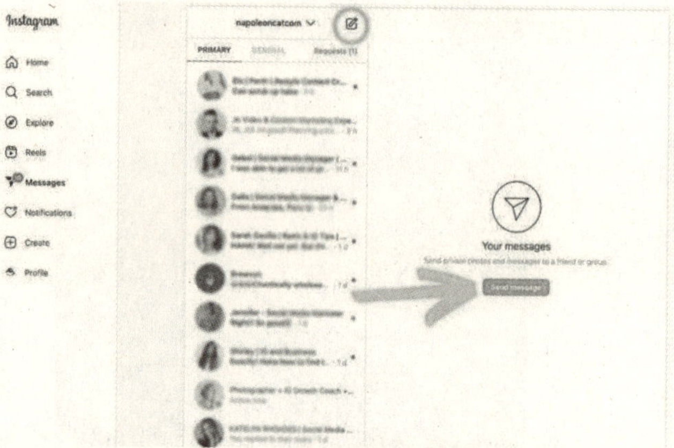

Image source: NapoleonCat.com[4]

e) Stories

Stories are temporary content that disappears after 24 hours, unless saved as Highlights. They support photos, videos, polls, Q and A, and links for eligible accounts. Stories appear at the top of the app and are presented chronologically.

Ideal for: Time-sensitive updates, behind-the-scenes glimpses, polls, product promotions, and audience engagement.

Image source: Sprout Social[5]

f) Highlights

Highlights are curated collections of Stories that remain permanently visible on your profile. They appear as circular icons below the bio section, allowing users to categorize and showcase key content.

Ideal for: Organizing evergreen content, product showcases, and quick access to important information.

Example: Highlight section of Fenty Beauty showcasing their products.

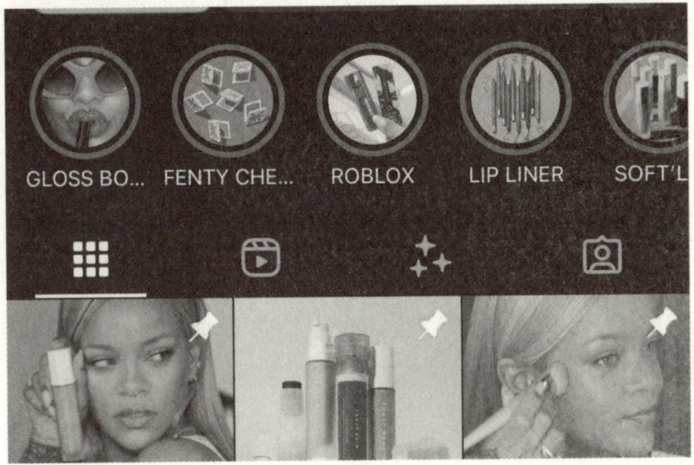

g) Channels

Channels are a broadcast feature for sharing text, photos, videos, and polls with followers who join the channel. Followers can react but cannot reply directly.

Ideal for: Exclusive updates, community engagement, and conducting polls.

Example: Dolly Singh creating her own Instagram community through channel.

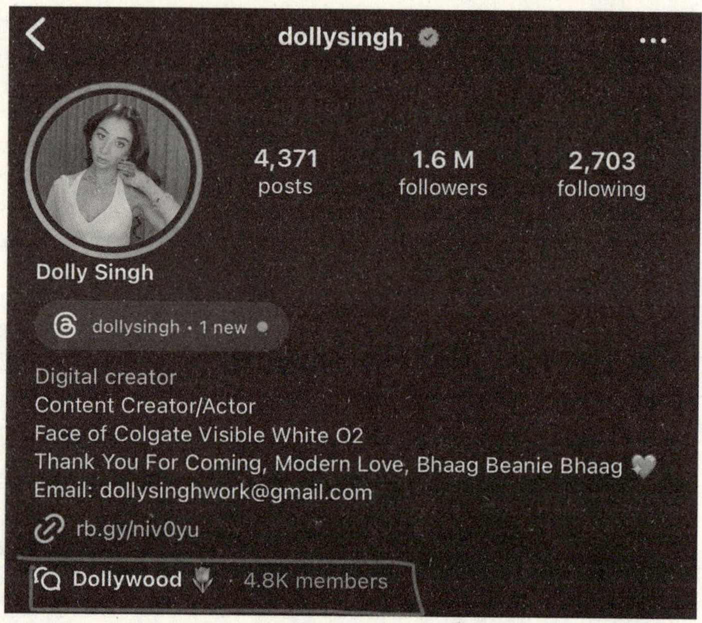

Image source: Dolly Singh[6]

h) Notes

Notes are short updates (up to sixty characters) displayed for 24 hours in followers' DMs. They encourage responses and initiate conversations.

Ideal for: Quick announcements, thoughts, or updates that spark interaction.

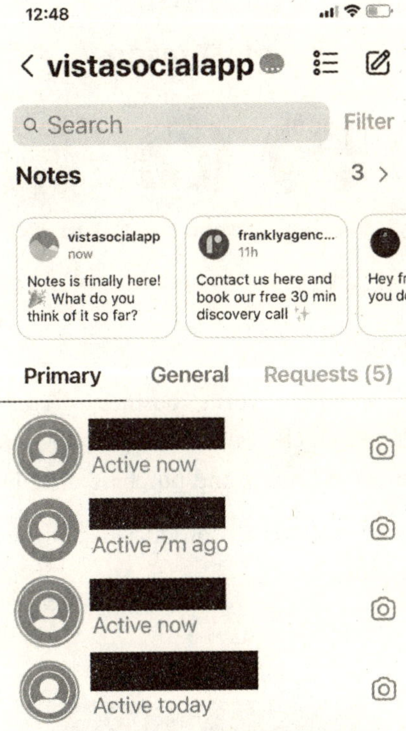

Image source: Vistasocial.com[7]

i) Live

Instagram Live enables real-time video broadcasts of up to four hours, allowing interaction through comments and reactions.

Ideal for: Hosting Q and A sessions, live events, interviews, and product launches.

Image source: Sprout Social[8]

j) Shopping

Instagram Shopping turns business accounts into virtual storefronts. Products can be tagged in posts and Stories, allowing users to browse and purchase directly within the app.

Ideal for: E-commerce, product catalogues, and creating shoppable content.

Image source: Bewakoof[9]

k) Ads

Instagram Ads promote content through various formats, including photo, video, carousel, Stories, and Reels ads. Ads are targeted based on audience demographics and behaviours.

Ideal for: Reaching new audiences, driving traffic, generating leads, and meeting marketing goals.

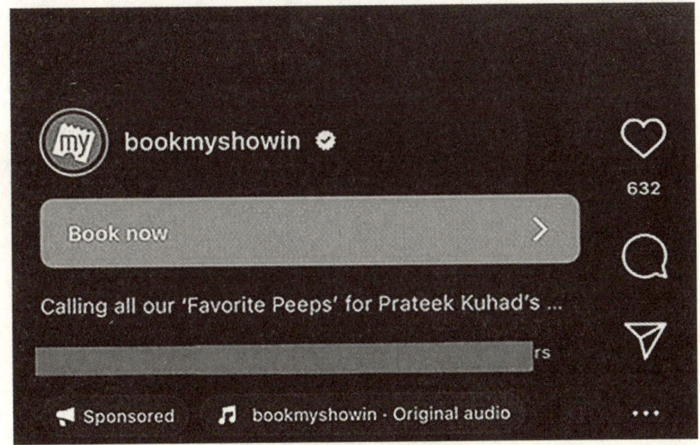

Image source: BookMyShow[10]

l) Collabs

Collabs allow up to four accounts to co-author a post or Reel. The content appears on all collaborators' profiles and shares engagement metrics.

Ideal for: Cross-promotion, influencer partnerships, and joint announcements.

Source: Sara Ali Khan's Instagram account[11]

m) Close Friends

Close Friends enables sharing Stories with a selected group. Stories shared this way have a green ring, and are visible only to the chosen audience.

Ideal for: Exclusive or personal content, testing ideas, and creating a sense of exclusivity.

6.1.2 Inspire—with Content

The 'Inspire' in the L.I.F.T. framework focuses on creating content that aligns with your audience and drives action. You want to create engaging, resourceful content that encourages your followers to interact, share, and respond.

Creating inspiring content on Instagram means cutting through the noise and touching people's hearts in a world that often feels overwhelming. It's about sharing stories that make people pause mid-scroll, take a deep breath, and think, 'Yeah, I needed that today.'

In a world of endless scrolling and dropping attention, these are the posts that stick with you. They're shared in group chats, discussed over coffee, and remembered long after you've closed the app. They remind us that behind every screen is a real person with real struggles and triumphs.

These content pieces on Instagram capture attention, evoke emotion, and compel users to take the next step—whether that's in the form of likes, comments, shares, or making a purchase. Here are a few types of content that I have seen work the best on the platform.

a) Visual Storytelling

Visual storytelling uses Instagram's very nature to create narratives that captivate and engage viewers. It combines photos, videos, and text overlays to craft cohesive stories like transformations, day-in-the-life content, or product journeys.

Effect: Visual storytelling evokes emotions and helps users experience things virtually, inspiring actions and leaving a lasting impact.

b) Educational Content

Educational content provides insights, tutorials, or valuable information. Popular formats include carousel posts for step-by-step guides, infographics for data, and Reels for short video lessons.

Effect: This content simplifies learning, making complex topics approachable. It positions brands as knowledgeable and provides followers with value, enhancing credibility.

c) Funny Content

Humour cuts through the noise with memes, witty captions, or relatable video sketches. Leveraging cultural references and trending audio enhances shareability and reach.

Effect: Funny content entertains, humanizes brands, and fosters loyalty, creating a lasting connection with audiences while boosting engagement.

d) Cause-Related Content

Cause-related posts align with social, environmental, or charitable values, showcasing a brand's commitment to meaningful causes. Examples include sustainability practices or highlighting ethical business operations.

Effect: This content builds emotional connections, showing that the brand cares about societal issues. It fosters trust and a sense of shared purpose among followers.

e) Authenticity

Authentic content highlights genuine, unfiltered moments, such as candid photos, personal reflections, or raw behind-the-scenes looks. It emphasizes imperfections and honest storytelling.

Effect: Authenticity builds trust and credibility, fostering deeper emotional connections and long-term loyalty.

f) Behind-the-Scenes

Behind-the-scenes (BTS) content offers an inside look at operations, such as product development, creative processes, or team dynamics. It reveals the effort behind the scenes.

Effect: This kind of content creates transparency, showcasing the human side of the brand and strengthening audience empathy and loyalty.

g) Trending Topics

Trending topics capitalize on viral conversations and popular challenges. Participating in trends, such as using trending audio or hashtags, increases visibility and relevance.

Effect: Joining trends boosts engagement and positions your brand as current and relatable, encouraging interaction and social sharing.

h) Interactive Posts

Interactive posts actively engage users with features like polls, question stickers, quizzes, and sliders in Stories. Posts prompting actions like 'Tag a friend' or 'Comment below' also fall into this category.

Effect: These posts increase engagement and visibility. Instagram rewards interactive content by amplifying its reach, turning your brand into a vibrant part of the platform's community.

What Type of Content Should You Create?

Let's look at a couple of real-life examples of approaches you can customize and use for three typical objectives.

Building Your Start-up

Sleepy Owl Coffee started their small Delhi-based start-up in 2016, founded by three friends who wanted to take India's coffee scene up a notch. Since then, they've been all the rage on social media, especially Instagram. The brand uses edutainment Reels to show off easy brew recipes and latte art tutorials, making fancy coffee seem doable at everybody's home.

Their stories take followers behind the scenes on how they make their cold brew and other coffees, building brand trust through transparency.

Image source: Sleepy Owl Coffee's Instagram page highlighting their tutorials for baristas at home[12]

Sleepy Owl gets creative with Instagram's interactive features, using polls to let followers vote on new flavours and the 'Add Yours' sticker for a daily 'Morning Coffee Views' thread. This strategy has turned their followers into a fanbase community of coffee lovers. Their IGTV series (now Reels) 'Brew it Yourself' has become a go-to space for coffee lovers, skyrocketing the engagement. By mixing educational content with relatable coffee humour, Sleepy Owl has grown from a small start-up to a recognized brand, proving that good content can be as addictive as caffeine.

Building Your Company's Brand

- Share industry insights and trends through informative carousel posts.

- Create product showcase Reels highlighting key features and benefits.

- Share company milestones and achievements through celebratory posts.

- Produce behind-the-scenes Stories showing your company culture and work environment.
- Develop 'Meet the Team' posts to humanize your brand.
- Create tutorial content, demonstrating how to use your products or services.
- Share customer success stories and testimonials as image posts or short video clips.
- Post user-generated content featuring your products to build social proof.
- Create 'A Day in the Life' content following different roles within your company.

Brand story: Nike has been ruling the streets of Instagram as their reputation precedes the company. The brand has been leveraging the platform's features to create impactful campaigns that go beyond traditional advertising.

One such example was their 'Equality Campaign', where they used Reels, Stories and carousel posts to drive engagement and develop a sense of community.

Through Reels, they shared powerful clips featuring athletes like LeBron James and Serena Williams, blending strong visuals with emotive storytelling that resonated deeply with their audience.

Using Instagram Stories, Nike offered behind-the-scenes insights, interviews, and event highlights, while incorporating interactive elements like polls to encourage real-time dialogue. This strategic use of Instagram features not only amplified their message, but also engaged followers on a personal level, turning their social justice campaign into a multi-dimensional experience that sparked conversation and became a driving force for actionable results.

Image source: Nike's equality campaign, 2017[13]

Building Personal Brand

- Share your expertise through quick tips and advice in carousel posts.

- Share your daily routine or work process through day-in-the-life content.

- Use Reels to showcase your personality and create relatable content.

- Use polls and question stickers in Stories to engage with your audience.

- Share your journey—including both successes and setbacks—in longer captions.

- Collaborate with other professionals in your field through Instagram Live.

- Create a series of posts or Stories Highlights that dive deep into your area of expertise.

- Consistently use personal branding elements like specific colours or fonts.

Personal brand story: Whenever we think of a relatable content creator in the Indian industry, we hear the name Dolly Singh. She has successfully established herself as a prominent personal brand on

Instagram by creatively utilizing a range of features. Her Instagram Reels are famously known to showcase her comedic sketches, which often highlight relatable situations and characters in life, resonating with a wide audience.

Her Instagram Stories are a key component of her engagement strategy, as she uses them for interactive content like polls, Q and As, and behind-the-scenes glimpses, fostering a sense of community with her followers. Additionally, Dolly takes advantage of Instagram Live to connect with her audience in real-time, discussing various topics and sharing insights.

By collaborating with brands and fellow creators, she utilizes the collaboration feature to broaden her reach and enhance her visibility. Through these various Instagram features, Dolly's authenticity and humour shine, making her a beloved figure in the digital landscape.

Image source: Dolly Singh's Instagram page

6.1.3 Focus—on Positioning

Taking a cue from the ancient Greek philosopher Plato one can say that each man is capable of doing one thing well. If he attempts several, he will fail to achieve distinction in any.

'Focus' in the L.I.F.T. framework reinforces clarity and intention in your Instagram strategy. It means identifying and emphasizing the key elements that make your brand unique, and appealing to your target audience.

In the fast-paced world of social media, brands often find themselves jumping from one trend to another, adopting every new 'strategy' they hear without really analysing whether it aligns with their core values or audience expectations. This 'we are there everywhere' approach can dilute their message, confuse followers, and ultimately lead to a loss of brand identity.

Focus acts as a filter, helping you decide:

- What type of content to create.
- How to present it.
- When to post it.
- Whom to target.

A focused approach eliminates distractions and creates a cohesive Instagram presence that stands out in a crowded market. From my experience working with various brands, brands with a clear focus consistently outperform those with a scattered approach. They achieve higher engagement rates and faster growth, ultimately building a clear brand identity.

So, what exactly do you need to focus on?

a) Brand Message

Your brand message is the core of who you are and what you stand for. Identify three to five key values, craft a concise mission statement, and ensure every post aligns with your themes. Use consistent language and tone. Regularly revisit and refine your message to reflect your brand's evolution.

b) Target Audience

Understand your audience beyond demographics. Use Instagram Insights, comments, and DMs to learn their preferences and challenges. Tailor content to address their pain points and interests using relatable language and references.

c) Content Pillars

Define three to five main topics that align with your brand and audience interests. Build a content calendar to maintain balance and consistency. Develop recurring series for each pillar, and regularly evaluate their performance to adapt as needed.

d) Posting Consistency

Establish a realistic, sustainable posting schedule (daily, weekly, etc.). Use tools like Hootsuite to plan and maintain consistency, focusing on quality over quantity. Stick to content standards to avoid burnout and maintain engagement.

e) Aesthetic

Create a recognizable visual identity with a consistent colour palette, editing style, and branded elements like logos or templates. Plan your feed layout for visual harmony, balancing polished content with authentic, relatable posts.

6.1.4 Track—your Performance

'Tracking' in the L.I.F.T. framework means monitoring your Instagram performance through data and defined metrics. This allows you to understand what's working, what isn't, and how to improve.

Without tracking, you're essentially operating in the dark. I've seen countless strategies fail because they weren't backed by data. You can spend endless hours speculating what's working and what's not, but let the data speak for itself. It's the ultimate guide to understanding what's effective and what's just noise.

Regular tracking leads to informed decisions, better content, and ultimately, faster growth.

While there are many quantitative and qualitative metrics you can look at, it's best to keep things simple and focus on KPIs that are direct determinants. I recommend tracking these metrics:

- **Reach**

  This shows how many unique accounts have seen your post. It's a good indicator of your content's visibility. If your reach is low, it might be time to reassess your hashtags or posting times.

- **Impressions**

  This shows the total number of times your post was viewed, including multiple views from the same account. A high impression count relative to your reach suggests your content is compelling enough for people to view it multiple times.

- **Profile Visits**

  This indicates how many times users visited your profile from a specific post. It's useful for understanding which types of content drive the most interest in your brand.

- **Engagement**

  This includes likes, comments, saves, and shares. It's the most important metric because it shows how your audience interacts with your content. In my experience, a high engagement rate often correlates with account growth and increased reach.

- **Website Clicks**

  If you have a link in your bio, this metric shows how many users clicked it. It helps in understanding how effectively you're driving traffic from Instagram to your website.

- **Follower Growth**

  This tracks the number of new followers gained (or lost) over time. While not the be-all-end-all metric, steady follower growth usually indicates you're creating content that people like and want to interact with.

- **Reels Metrics**

  For Reels, you can see plays, likes, comments, saves, and shares. These metrics help you gauge which Reels formats or topics perform best with your audience. Based on this, you can create more relevant Instagram content even in other formats.

- **Story Metrics**

  For Stories, you can track exits (how many people leave your story), replies, and sticker taps. These metrics help you understand how engaging your Stories are and which elements work the best.

How Often Should You Review These Metrics?

I say weekly at a minimum. Look for patterns—which types of posts get the most engagement; or what times of day see the highest reach. Use these insights to refine your Instagram strategy.

But please remember, numbers without context are just numbers. Always connect your metrics back to your overall Instagram goals to ensure you're tracking what truly matters for your brand's success. For instance, if you're looking to drive sales, it matters less if your posts are getting a lot of likes but there's very little conversion.

Note: You can even use third-party analytics that help you track and monitor your Instagram performance more conveniently and with better insights. I'll discuss more on using third-party tools later in this chapter.

6.2 Closing Note

Instagram is fundamental to business success for those serious about online growth. The platform offers great opportunities for brand building, lead generation, and sales. While growing on Instagram is challenging, everything I've discussed in this chapter will get you started with the right insights and strategy.

Apply the L.I.F.T. framework to build your foundation. Test different content types and engagement tactics. Keep an eye on trends like AI content creation and immersive experiences. And, most importantly, focus on providing value and building genuine connections with your audience. These, when consistently applied, will help you leverage Instagram's full potential and grow faster.

6.3 A Quick Checklist to Get You Started

- ✓ Collaborate with influencers or brands to expand your reach.
- ✓ Set a clear Instagram goal (e.g., brand awareness, lead generation).
- ✓ Choose a professional and easy to recognize display picture.
- ✓ Optimize your bio with a concise message and call-to-action.
- ✓ Add a strategic link in your bio (consider using Linktree for multiple links).
- ✓ Ensure your username is consistent with your brand identity.
- ✓ Follow key industry leaders, competitors, and relevant hashtags.
- ✓ Define three to five content pillars aligned with your brand.
- ✓ Create a content calendar to plan your posts in advance.

✓ Develop a consistent visual aesthetic (colour palette, editing style).

✓ Post a mix of Reels, Stories, and carousels to engage your audience.

✓ Set up Story Highlights for important and evergreen content.

✓ Engage with followers by responding to comments and DMs.

✓ Leverage Instagram's features like Live sessions.

7

The Social Saga: Facebook, YouTube, LinkedIn, X, and More

As a start-up, every decision with respect to marketing is critical; every missed opportunity may seem like a potential setback. But in reality, spreading yourself too thin is the fastest way to burn out. You have to know what your goals are, what is your target group, what their behaviour pattern is, which platforms they visit to consume content, and on the basis of that, you can decide the right mix of social media platforms for your business.

In 2023, we had the opportunity to work with Rohit, a gym owner in Mumbai. Despite his best efforts, Rohit was struggling to attract new members. Here's what he had been doing:

- For three months, Rohit had been consistently posting high-quality workout videos and transformation photos on Instagram.

- He had invested significant time and resources into creating engaging content, but unfortunately, it hadn't yielded the desired results.

Rohit's Instagram efforts had generated almost no tangible results. His follower count was stagnant, and engagement was limited. More importantly, his gym's membership numbers remained unchanged.

We recommended that Rohit shift his focus from Instagram to building an engaged Facebook Group for his neighbourhood fitness enthusiasts. Here's what we did:

- Created a private Facebook Group exclusively for people living in Rohit's neighbourhood who were interested in fitness.
- Designed an engaging content strategy that included workout tips, nutrition advice, and motivational stories.
- Encouraged group members to share their own fitness journeys, successes, and challenges.
- Hosted live Q and A sessions and workshops within the group to foster a sense of community.

In less than two months, Rohit's gym saw a remarkable 40 per cent surge in membership. The Facebook Group had become a vibrant community of like-minded individuals who were passionate about fitness. Here are some key statistics:

- Group membership grew from 0 to 500+ members in just six weeks.
- Engagement rates soared, with an average of 50+ comments and reactions per post.
- The group became a lead-generation machine, with numerous members expressing interest in joining Rohit's gym.

Then there's Priya, who runs a B2B software company in Bengaluru. She spent six months pushing content on Facebook, Instagram, and X (formerly Twitter). Money down the drain! One well-planned LinkedIn campaign later, she landed three enterprise clients worth INR 50 lakh each.

You will face the same choice today. Which platforms deserve your time? Where will you find your customers? The answer isn't 'be everywhere'—that's terrible advice. Your time and money are limited. You need a strategic approach to pick the right platforms.

This chapter will show you exactly how to make that choice. I'll discuss:

- The C.A.S.T. Matrix to find right mix of social media platforms.

- How to maximize the potential ROI from efforts on social media marketing.

- Tactics to dominate these social media platforms.

Let us start with the basics.

7.1 Understanding Social Platform Differentiation

Each social media platform serves a different purpose. I have seen many founders make two common mistakes: trying to be everywhere, and choosing platforms based on user count alone. Let me explain why both approaches fail.

Remember what happened to Indian TikTok creators in 2020? Overnight, the platform got banned, and creators who built their entire business on TikTok lost everything. That's why putting all your eggs in one basket is risky. However, spreading yourself too thin across all platforms is equally problematic.

Take our client Ravindra Chaudhary from Delhi. His team of three tried managing Facebook, Instagram, LinkedIn, YouTube, and X simultaneously. They ended up with mediocre content everywhere and zero business impact. We cut it down to just LinkedIn and YouTube. Their leads tripled in two months.

Most founders look at user numbers and jump to conclusions. Yes, Facebook dominates globally with over three billion monthly active users. YouTube follows with 2.5 billion, and Instagram has two billion. These numbers look impressive.

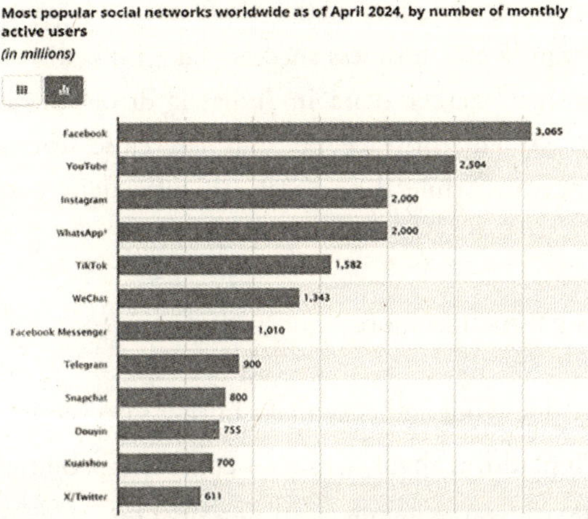

Image source: Statista.com, 2024

In India, the story is similar, yet different. Facebook commands 55.46 per cent of social media traffic, followed by Instagram at around 40 per cent. YouTube and X lag significantly behind, each holding less than 10 per cent market share.

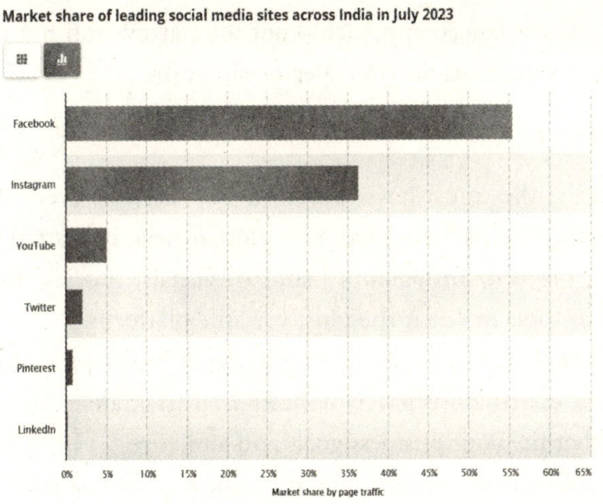

Image source: Statista.com, 2023

But these numbers do not tell the whole story. A large user base does not always translate to business success. Take LinkedIn, for example. Despite minimal market share in India, it drives the highest B2B conversions. My enterprise clients routinely close seven-figure deals through LinkedIn, while their Facebook campaigns barely generate leads.

Here is what matters more:

- Where does your audience make business decisions?
- Which platform aligns with your content capabilities?
- Where can you maintain consistent quality?

I'll share a real example. Meesho sellers focus heavily on WhatsApp and Facebook because that's where their target customers (women in Tier-3 cities) spend time. However, a SaaS company selling to enterprise CTOs would waste resources there; its audience makes buying decisions on LinkedIn and YouTube, consuming thought leadership content and detailed product demos.

You need a balanced approach—not too narrow and not too wide. The right mix depends on your specific situation.

Instagram + 1

Instagram is the must-have platform for almost every business. Whether you're in fashion, manufacturing, fitness, industrial supplies, education, or tech, Instagram's blend of visuals, Stories, Reels, and engagement tools makes it the most versatile platform.

I've covered Instagram marketing in detail in the previous chapter because it's essential. What you need is 'Instagram + 1'—another platform that fits your business goals and audience.

In the subsequent sections, I'll explain how to choose your '+1'. But first, let's understand these other platforms.

What Platforms Are Available to You?

Each social media platform caters to different types of users and businesses. You need to understand what makes each platform unique, so you can use them optimally to build a brand and drive sales.

Let us look at the ten most popular platforms. I'll help you understand what they're good for, who's using them, and why they might—or might not—be suitable for you. This comparison highlights the unique strengths of each platform, helping you choose the best fit for your business goals.

1. Visual-Centric

- Instagram: Ideal for B2C, local businesses, and visual storytelling.
- TikTok: Short-form video content for Gen Z.
- Pinterest: Visual inspiration for home decor, fashion, and art.

2. Professional Networking

- LinkedIn: B2B marketing, thought leadership, and professional networking.

3. Real-Time Conversations

- X: Ideal for real-time updates, news, and thought leadership.
- Threads: Conversational marketing and community engagement.

4. Community-Building

- Facebook: Local community-based services, events, and lifestyle brands.
- WhatsApp: Personal connections and community engagement.
- Telegram: Building broadcast channels and niche communities.

5. Educational Content

- YouTube: In-depth video content for education, SaaS, and technology.

7.2 The C.A.S.T. Matrix to Pick the Best Social Platforms

Choosing the right social media platforms for your business can be tricky. With so many options, where do you start? I've already mentioned that Instagram is a must. You need to pick one more platform—your '+1'.

This is where the C.A.S.T. Matrix comes in. My team uses this framework for all our big-ticket clients, to determine which additional platform will deliver the highest ROI for their business.

What Is the C.A.S.T. Matrix?

The C.A.S.T. Matrix helps you decide which social media platforms will deliver the highest ROI for your business. It evaluates each platform against four key criteria: Clarity, Audience, Scope, and Time.

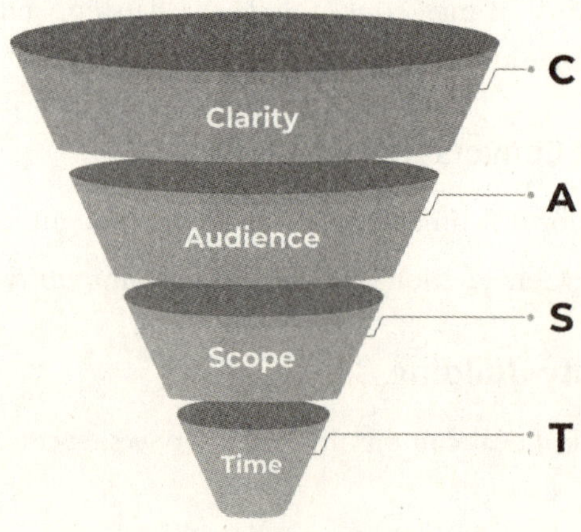

The C.A.S.T. Matrix

Image source: Author's illustration

You score each platform on a scale of 1 to 5 for each of these factors. Add up the scores, and you'll see which platforms deserve your focus, and which you can afford to ignore.

This matrix ensures you avoid spreading yourself too thin and wasting resources on platforms that aren't effective for your goals. It brings clarity to your social strategy, making it more streamlined and efficient.

How to Use the C.A.S.T. Matrix?

7.2.1 Clarity—Understanding Your Goals

The first step is 'clarity'. Before diving into any platform, you need to know what you're trying to achieve.

Ask yourself, what is the specific outcome I want from being on this platform? It could be anything from brand awareness to lead generation, or from sales to customer service.

Let's say you run a B2B consultancy. LinkedIn is the right fit, if your goal is to establish thought leadership and connect with other industry experts.

But if you manage a neighbourhood bakery in Pune, your focus might be on reaching local customers and sharing updates on offers and events, which makes Facebook the better platform.

Scoring Clarity is about understanding how well each platform aligns with your unique business goals. If the platform perfectly supports your goal, give it a high score. If it seems disconnected from your goal, give it a lower score.

- **Score 5**: The platform perfectly matches your business goal.
- **Score 3**: The platform could help, but it's not ideal.
- **Score 1**: No clear alignment with your objectives.

7.2.2 Audience—Are They Even There?

Next, you need to determine if your 'audience' is present on the platform that you're considering. You can't just follow the crowd; you need to know that your customers are there and actively engaging.

If your audience is not present on a particular platform, your efforts are unlikely to yield results.

Imagine you are selling luxury kitchenware. In that case, Pinterest would be ideal, since users visit it for inspiration and are often ready to make decisions. On the other hand, if you're targeting business executives, they are more likely to be on LinkedIn than browsing for inspiration on Pinterest.

To score Audience, consider how well the platform aligns with where your customers spend their time. Are your customers engaged here, or would you be talking into a void?

- **Score 5**: Your target audience is very active on this platform.
- **Score 3**: Some of your audience is there, but it's not their main platform.
- **Score 1**: Your customers are almost entirely absent from this platform.

7.2.3 Scope—Can You Manage It Well?

Scope refers to the resources you have available. Do you realistically have the ability to produce content for this platform consistently?

This factor often trips founders up, because they underestimate how much effort certain platforms require. The goal is not just to be present but to be on the platform, understand more about the audience's behaviour and expectations, and create content accordingly to add value.

Let us say you are a start-up with a small team. You might want to be active on YouTube, Facebook, LinkedIn, and X. But video production for YouTube demands time, skills, and budget. If those aren't available, YouTube might get a low score in terms of Scope.

Meanwhile, WhatsApp could score higher if creating group messages and exclusive announcements suits your content capabilities.

To score Scope, consider whether your team can consistently create and post high-quality content. If you have the skills, time, and budget to produce content effectively, it deserves a high score.

- **Score 5**: You have the resources to create quality content regularly.

- **Score 3**: You can manage with a little stretch, but it won't be easy.

- **Score 1**: You're under-resourced for creating content on this platform.

7.2.4 Time—How Much Effort Does It Take?

The final factor is time. Different platforms have different time demands—some need you to be engaged throughout the day, while others require less frequent but still consistent effort.

You need to be honest about how much time you and your team can realistically commit.

Let's take an example. If you're managing social media alone, X may be challenging because it requires frequent posts and constant interaction to stay relevant.

In contrast, Pinterest may be more manageable, because it allows for less frequent, high-quality content that stays relevant longer.

Scoring for Time involves assessing if the time required to be successful on the platform is feasible for you. If the platform fits comfortably within your available hours, it should score high.

- **Score 5**: You have enough time to manage the platform without strain.

- **Score 3**: It will take some effort, but you can manage with careful planning.

- **Score 1**: The time requirement is far beyond what you can handle.

7.3 C.A.S.T. Matrix in Action

Let's take an example of a small fitness coaching business in Mumbai. You're considering platforms like Facebook, YouTube, LinkedIn, and Snapchat. Here's how the C.A.S.T. Matrix might help you decide:

Platform	Clarity (Goals)	Audience	Scope (Resources)	Time Commitment	Total Score
Facebook	5	5	4	4	18
YouTube	4	3	2	2	11
LinkedIn	3	2	3	4	12
Snapchat	4	4	5	4	17

Interpretation

- Facebook scores the highest at 18. For a fitness coaching business, Facebook is ideal for building connections with local audiences, sharing workout routines, and engaging directly through posts and community groups.

- Snapchat comes in at 17. Snapchat works well if you want to create content targeted at a younger audience who loves seeing short, spontaneous clips. It allows you to give a personal touch to your coaching through behind-the-scenes visuals, or daily motivational snippets.

- YouTube scores lower because video production demands time, effort, and editing capabilities that your small team might not have right now. It's better to invest in platforms that are more manageable for your current resources.

- LinkedIn doesn't have the perfect audience fit for your type of business, but it could work if you decide to expand your services to corporate wellness programmes, or position yourself as a thought leader in fitness and health.

The C.A.S.T. Matrix is all about focusing your resources where they count. Use this framework to clearly evaluate each platform's fit for your business, so you can avoid spreading yourself too thin and instead build an impactful social media presence.

7.4 Deep Dive: The Big Four

No matter which platform you've finalized based on this matrix, I want to spend some time discussing the top-four platforms that collectively get billions of daily users.

Understanding these platforms will help optimize your social media ROI—and prepare you for when you will eventually get more aggressive about multi-channel growth.

7.4.1 LinkedIn

LinkedIn values professional discussions and rewards content that fosters meaningful industry conversations.

Text posts around 1,300 characters in length perform best, with the first two lines being critical to grab attention. Document posts, like carousels for reports or guides, see high engagement, as do short, captioned videos under three minutes.

Articles are excellent for deep analysis, while newsletters keep your audience updated and notified. The algorithm favours fresh, original content, and measures success by engagement quality, time spent on posts, and relevance.

Hashtags matter here—stick to three to five relevant ones—and avoid external links, which reduce visibility.

7.4.2 X

X thrives on real-time conversations and trending topics, with content lifespans often limited to minutes. Quick, authentic updates and media-rich posts like images, videos, and GIFs perform well.

For extended narratives threads are great, while polls and Spaces (live audio discussions) boost interaction. Timing is everything on X—posts peak within the first 30 minutes, so consistent posting (three to four times daily) is key.

Unlike Instagram, X performs better with just one or two relevant hashtags. Personality driven communication resonates most with its audience.

7.4.3 Facebook

Facebook excels at building engaged communities. Visual content, including videos and live streams, outperforms other formats, with live videos generating six times more interactions.

Groups and events create dedicated spaces for interaction, while tools like Guides and Watch Parties help curate content and drive participation.

For businesses, Shop and Messenger integrations streamline e-commerce and customer service, while detailed insights and custom audience features optimize campaigns.

Facebook's algorithm prioritizes meaningful engagement, making it a strong platform for B2C brands and local businesses.

7.4.4 YouTube

YouTube uniquely combines social networking with powerful search capabilities, making it an excellent platform for evergreen content.

Videos focused on education, in-depth product reviews, or authentic storytelling perform particularly well. Thumbnails, video chapters, end screens, and playlists enhance user experience and encourage longer watch times.

YouTube's algorithm favours viewer retention and session length over recency, making SEO essential—titles, descriptions, tags, and transcripts—all play a role. Live streaming stands out here, as streams often gain replay value, making them perfect for tutorials and product launches.

Consistency matters; channels with clear content pillars are more likely to be recommended to relevant audiences.

7.5 You Know Which Platforms... Now What?

You have identified your 'Instagram + 1' platform using the C.A.S.T. Matrix. Now, it's time to build an actionable plan to leverage these platforms for maximum results. Here's how you can proceed with clarity and impact.

7.5.1 Define Platform-Specific Goals

Each social platform serves a different audience with distinct behaviours. So, you need clear and tailored goals for each to be successful.

For example, if Facebook is your '+1' platform, your goal might be to build an engaged local community and drive foot traffic to your store.

If LinkedIn is your +1, the goal could be to establish your brand as a thought leader and attract B2B leads. Defining these clear goals will keep your efforts focused.

So, how exactly do you set platform goals?

Identify the Primary Objective

For each platform, ask yourself, 'What is the most important outcome I want from this platform?' It could be brand awareness, driving sales, building a community, or generating leads.

Understand the Platform's Nature

Think about what makes each platform unique and how users engage there. Some platforms are community focused, others are for learning, and some are for showcasing expertise. Here's a quick overview of what makes each platform unique and how users generally engage there:

- **Facebook**: Ideal for building community and fostering local connections. Great for B2C businesses engaging directly with customers through groups and events.

- **YouTube**: Best for showcasing expertise through videos. Ideal for in-depth content like tutorials, thought leadership, and educational material.

- **WhatsApp**: Perfect for nurturing customer relationships through direct communication. Great for personal messaging, broadcast lists, and maintaining close customer contact.

- **TikTok** (for non-India markets): Strong at increasing brand visibility, particularly with younger audiences. Excellent for viral, short-form video content using trends and challenges.

- **Snapchat**: Targets younger audiences with ephemeral content. Great for brand awareness campaigns using behind-the-scenes videos or short, casual snippets.

- **X**: Ideal for positioning your brand in real-time industry conversations. Perfect for thought leadership, trends, and creating a dynamic brand voice.

- **Telegram**: Effective for building exclusive communities. Works well for sharing updates, exclusive content, and engaging with users on specific interests.
- **Pinterest**: Works well for inspiring potential customers, particularly with visual content. Effective for driving website traffic from users in a planning or discovery phase.

7.5.2 Align Goals with Your Target Audience

Set goals that consider where your audience is most likely to engage and take action. For example, the same audience might want to consume information differently on YouTube than on X.

Defining goals in this platform-specific way is important, because it helps you allocate resources effectively. You'll know exactly what kind of content to create, which audiences to target, and which metrics to track. It makes everything about your social media more intentional and purpose-driven.

7.5.3 Content Strategy for Each Platform

When creating content for your social platforms, each has a different style, audience, and type of content that works best.

So, you should tailor your content accordingly for specific platforms. I will cover some broad social media content tips you can apply to your Instagram + 1 strategy, regardless of the platform, in section 7.5.5.

7.5.4 Know Your Audience and Their Preferences

The first rule of creating engaging content is to know who you're talking to. Each platform attracts different demographics and behaviour patterns. For instance:

- On LinkedIn, users expect professional and educational content, while on Snapchat, users enjoy casual, fun, and behind-the-scenes footage.

- Facebook and Telegram attract communities, so content that encourages group participation—polls, interactive questions, or community spotlights—will work well.

Always adjust your content style to fit the audience's mindset on each platform.

7.5.5 Diversify Your Content Formats

It's important to mix up your content formats to keep your audience engaged. Here's a broad look at content types and how you can use them effectively across all platforms:

- **Video**: Video content is highly engaging across almost all platforms. Short, vertical videos perform well on platforms like TikTok, Snapchat, and Instagram Stories, while longer educational videos excel on YouTube and even LinkedIn.

- **Text posts**: Use short, snappy text posts to make points or spark engagement. X is perfect for quick thoughts and industry commentary, while Facebook and LinkedIn are good for more thoughtful posts or storytelling.

- **Visuals**: Infographics, behind-the-scenes photos, or user-generated content work well for platforms like Instagram, Pinterest, and Snapchat. High-quality visuals are key to stopping users as they scroll.

- **Live content**: If possible, consider live sessions—Facebook Live or YouTube Live—where you can interact directly with your audience. This is especially useful for Q and A sessions, launching new products, or offering exclusive insights.

7.5.6 Repurpose, Don't Reuse

One of the biggest mistakes is duplicating the same content across multiple platforms. Repurposing is different—it means taking the core of your content and adapting it for each platform.

For example, if you create a long-form video for YouTube, pull a short clip from it for TikTok or Instagram Reels. Take the insights shared in that video and turn them into a text post for LinkedIn or X.

This ensures that every piece of content feels native to the platform it's posted on, while you still get more mileage out of your core material.

7.5.7 Optimize for Engagement

Engagement is key to social media growth and, is more important than the volume of content you put out. Here are ways to ensure high engagement:

- **Call to action**: Each piece of content should include a subtle CTA. For Facebook or Instagram, it could be 'Tag a friend who needs this!' On YouTube, ask viewers to 'Subscribe for more content'. Tailor your CTA to the type of engagement you're looking for, whether it's shares, comments, or direct clicks.

- **Interactive elements**: Platforms like Facebook, Instagram, and Telegram support interactive features. Use polls, quizzes, and Q and A sessions to encourage audience interaction.

- **Timing**: Post when your audience is most active. You can use the platform's analytics tools to identify these timeframes. Facebook Insights or YouTube Studio can help determine the ideal posting time based on when your audience is most engaged.

7.5.8 Stay Authentic and Add Value

Social media users quickly scroll past content that feels promotional or lacks personality. Instead, you should focus on adding value to your audience:

- **LinkedIn:** Share thought leadership that provides solutions to industry pain points.

- **Instagram or Pinterest:** Show creative ways to use your product, solve problems, or offer inspiration.

- **Telegram or WhatsApp:** Make the content feel exclusive—such as early product announcements or behind-the-scenes clips.

Authenticity goes a long way in building trust. Show the people behind the brand, celebrate your customer successes, and share challenges you've overcome. Relatability drives genuine engagement.

Note: Growth takes consistency, strategic action, and constant listening to what your audience wants. Apply these tactics, refine them based on your analytics, and build a community that is not just large in number, but actively engaged and truly connected to what you offer.

7.6 A Quick Checklist to Get Started

Here's a quick checklist to help you start implementing what you've learned, and build an impactful social media strategy from the ground up:

- ✓ Determine your business objectives for social media (e.g., lead generation, community building).

✓ Use the C.A.S.T. matrix to evaluate and pick your '+1' platform alongside Instagram.

✓ Score platforms for Clarity, Audience, Scope, and Time using the C.A.S.T. criteria.

✓ Define platform-specific goals for Instagram and your '+1', based on their unique strengths.

✓ Understand your target audience for each chosen platform, and how they interact there.

✓ Develop content ideas that align with your platform-specific goals.

✓ Plan a mix of content formats suitable for your chosen platforms (videos, visuals, text).

✓ Set up accounts on automation tools like Buffer for scheduling and Canva for designing.

✓ Establish key metrics to track success on each platform (e.g., engagement rate, follower growth)

✓ Create a monthly schedule to review platform performance and refine your strategy.

8

Recapturing Leaked Opportunities: Retargeting and Remarketing

'IS MARKETING NOT ENOUGH ALREADY THAT I NEED TO remarket? How does it make a difference?'

If you've been wondering about these questions, let's get your doubts cleared first.

You can pour millions into marketing, chasing visibility and clicks, but without remarketing and retargeting, most of it slips through the cracks. Studies show that approximately 93 per cent of first-time visitors leave a website without taking action, meaning potential leads vanish unless you strategically bring them back. Remarketing bridges this gap, reminding users why they came in the first place and nudging them to convert.

Here are two real-time examples to understand this game further.

Anil runs an online electronics store in Mumbai. His website attracts over 15,000 visitors every month, but his conversion rate is just 0.7 per cent. Despite the heavy traffic, sales remained disappointingly low. After implementing retargeting ads that reminded visitors of the gadgets they had viewed, his conversion rate jumped to 2.5 per cent.

This simple strategy added an extra INR 3 lakh to his monthly revenue.

Meanwhile, Meera owns a boutique bakery in Jamshedpur with a loyal customer base. She noticed many customers ordered once for special occasions, but didn't return. To encourage repeat business, she launched a remarketing campaign, sending personalized emails with exclusive offers and showcasing new pastry collections. Within two months, her repeat orders increased by 40 per cent, boosting her quarterly profits by INR 2 lakh.

You might be facing similar challenges—high website traffic but low sales, or one-time customers who never come back. Retargeting and remarketing can bridge this gap.

In this chapter, I'll show you:

- The L.O.O.P. system my team uses to create high-converting retargeting and remarketing campaigns.
- Step-by-step implementation guides that you can start using today.
- Real tactics that work for both B2B and B2C businesses.

8.1 Understanding the Terminologies

Think of retargeting and remarketing as two different ways to bring back people who've shown interest in your business.

One of our clients runs a chain of luxury homestays in Shimla. They faced two different situations:

Situation 1: People visited their website, browsed through property photos, and checked available dates, but left without booking.

Situation 2: Previous guests needed to be brought back for another stay.

These represent the two concepts we're discussing.

Retargeting helps you reach website visitors based on their browsing behaviour. Through special tracking on your website, you can show these potential customers relevant ads across different platforms. This includes both new visitors and existing customers who browse your website—if you're tracking their behaviour through cookies, it's retargeting.

Remember when you checked out a resort online and suddenly saw ads for that exact property everywhere? That's retargeting in action.

Image source: Semrush blog, 'What is retargeting and how does it work', 21 November 2023

Remarketing, on the other hand, focuses exclusively on your existing customers, using their contact information (typically email addresses). You upload your customer email list to platforms like Google Ads or Meta Ads, and they'll match these emails with user accounts. Now, you can show targeted ads to your past customers when they browse other websites, use social media, or check their Gmail. The key here is that remarketing only works with customer contact information, not browsing behaviour.

Here's an example of Grammarly promoting its premium plan to its existing users through email.

Image source: Semrush blog, 'Remarketing Campaign 101: Definition, Types, and Tips', 14 May 2024

I often see founders confuse these terms or use them interchangeably. While both strategies aim to increase bookings, they target different groups:

- **Retargeting**: Uses cookie-based tracking to reach anyone who visits your website (including existing customers), based purely on their browsing behaviour.

- **Remarketing**: Reaches only existing customers using their contact information (typically email addresses), regardless of whether they've visited your website recently.

Understanding this difference helps you create more effective campaigns. You'll need different messaging for someone who just browsed your website versus a past customer who already knows your service quality.

Let's look at the key differences in detail.

Aspect	Retargeting	Remarketing
Target audience	Website visitors who haven't purchased yet	Existing customers
Data used	Cookie-based tracking of website behaviour	Customer email list
Trigger point	Website visits, cart abandonment, product page views	Previous purchase history
Primary goal	Convert first-time visitors into customers	Drive repeat purchases from existing customers
Tracking method	Pixel/cookie tracking on website	Email-based customer list
Platforms used	All major ad platforms, like Meta, Google Ads, LinkedIn, and more	All major ad platforms, like Meta, Google Ads, LinkedIn, and more

8.2 The L.O.O.P. Framework

Most retargeting and remarketing campaigns fail because businesses treat them like regular ads. They show the same message to everyone, hope for the best, and wonder why results don't improve. I've seen this mistake cost companies thousands in ad spend with little to show for it.

You need a framework that works for both retargeting and remarketing. Over the years of running campaigns, we've used and highly benefitted from the L.O.O.P. framework:

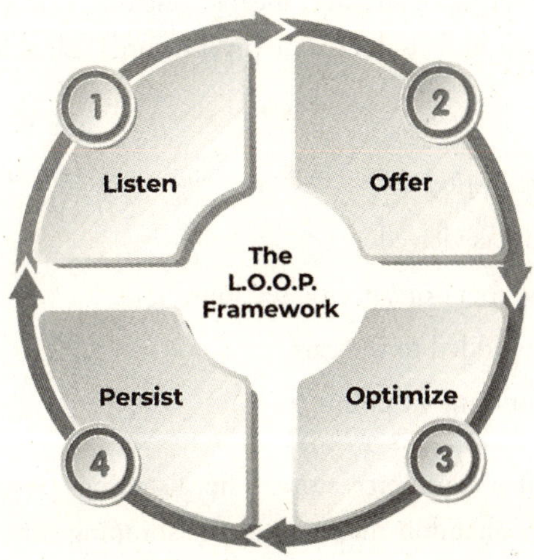

Image source: Author's illustration

What Does It Mean?

The L.O.O.P. system is a straightforward framework I've developed to help you create effective retargeting and remarketing campaigns. It stands for **Listen**, **Offer**, **Optimize**, and **Persist**. This system guides you through understanding your audience, crafting personalized offers, refining your strategies, and maintaining consistent engagement to drive conversions and build lasting customer relationships.

Let me break it down.

8.2.1 Listen

The foundation of any successful retargeting or remarketing campaign starts with listening. This means monitoring how users interact with your business across different touchpoints. Without understanding these interactions, you're essentially marketing in the dark.

In retargeting, listening means tracking website behaviour through pixels and cookies. The pixel records valuable information like:

- Pages visited
- Products viewed
- Time spent on specific sections
- Items added to the cart
- Abandonment points

Think of an e-commerce store. The 'listening' phase reveals that most visitors abandon their cart at the shipping information page. This insight tells you exactly what might be stopping potential customers from completing their purchases.

In remarketing, listening revolves around understanding your existing customers' behaviour, which helps tailor your messaging. Your focus stays on:

- Purchase patterns
- Product preferences
- Customer segments
- Response to previous campaigns
- Buying frequency

This listening phase doesn't just collect data—it helps you understand intent. Someone who spends five minutes reading your product specifications shows different intent than someone who quickly glances at your homepage and leaves.

It helps you to understand different buyer personas and their purchase habits to help you with better understanding about the type of ad content you can showcase.

For example, if people are spending quite some time in the review section of a particular product, you can target them with 'here's what people are saying about xyz' type of content.

The goal is much more than tracking users' actions. The goal is to understand why they do what they do. This understanding shapes every other aspect of your retargeting or remarketing strategy. When you truly listen to user behaviour, you can create messages that resonate rather than interrupt.

8.2.2 Offer

The 'Offer' phase transforms your audience insights into relevant messages. It's not just about discounts or promotions; the focus is on crafting content that speaks directly to user behaviour and intentions.

In retargeting, your offers align with the visitor's displayed interests. A user who viewed your product-pricing page needs different messaging than someone who just read your blog. The key is relevance—showing people exactly what caught their attention, enhanced with compelling reasons to return and convert.

For remarketing, offers build upon your existing relationship. Since these people already know your brand and have purchased before, your messaging focuses on value extension rather than introduction. This might mean showcasing new products similar to their past purchases, or highlighting advanced features they haven't tried yet.

The true power of the 'Offer' phase is in personalization. Generic messages like 'Come back!' or 'Buy now!' don't acknowledge your unique relationship with each segment of your audience. Instead, your offers should reflect:

- Previous interactions with your brand
- Specific products or services viewed
- Stage in the customer journey
- Past purchase behaviour (for remarketing)

Think of your offers as continuing a conversation rather than starting a new one. You're not interrupting people with random promotions—you're following up on interests they've already expressed.

By refining your offers to meet their expectations, you position yourself as a thoughtful problem-solver, not just another seller. It's about showing them that you understand their journey, and providing exactly what aligns with their interests at the right time. Instead of generic messaging, these strategies focus on presenting value-driven, relevant solutions, making your brand not just noticeable, but one that knows exactly what to say every time.

8.2.3 Optimize

The 'Optimize' phase focuses on continuous improvement of your campaigns based on real performance data. Raw data reveals what works and what needs adjustment in your retargeting and remarketing efforts.

For retargeting campaigns, optimization examines:

- Ad creative performance
- Message effectiveness
- Audience response rates
- Conversion patterns
- Cost efficiency

Each data point guides your refinement process. When specific creatives generate higher engagement, you'll understand which visual elements or messages resonate with your audience.

Similarly, conversion patterns highlight the most effective times and places to show your ads.

In remarketing, optimization centres on:

- Customer segment responses
- Message effectiveness across segments
- Timing of repeat purchases
- Campaign ROI
- Customer lifetime value trends

Data-driven optimization removes guesswork from your campaigns. Numbers tell the story of what your audience prefers. A drop in engagement might signal message fatigue. A spike in conversions could highlight a particularly effective offer.

The optimization phase turns good campaigns into great ones through systematic refinement. Small improvements compound over time to create significant results. Regular analysis and adjustment ensure your campaigns stay relevant and effective.

8.2.4 Persist

The 'Persist' phase establishes your long-term connection with potential and existing customers. Marketing success requires consistent presence and patience. Many businesses give up too soon, missing valuable conversion opportunities.

In retargeting, persistence means maintaining visibility throughout the customer decision journey. People rarely make purchase decisions instantly. For better understanding, put yourself in the customer's shoes. How do you make purchases generally? How do your family members do it differently? This will help you identify at least four or five different purchase behaviours.

Most customers research, compare and consider before buying. Your campaigns should mirror this natural decision-making process through:

- Varied messaging at different stages
- Strategic ad frequency
- Multiple touchpoint presence
- Consistent brand voice

Remarketing persistence focuses on staying relevant to existing customers without overwhelming them. Your previous customers already know your brand. They need well-timed reminders and value-adding messages that:

- Respect their buying cycles
- Acknowledge their past interactions
- Maintain brand connection
- Add genuine value

Strategic persistence differs from mere repetition. Every message should move the conversation forward. Think of persistence as an ongoing dialogue where each interaction builds upon previous ones.

The true power of persistence emerges when combined with the other elements of the L.O.O.P. system. You listen to understand your audience, create relevant offers, optimize your approach, and persist with proven strategies.

Note: The real power of the L.O.O.P. system is its cyclical nature. Each component feeds into the next, creating a continuous improvement cycle for your campaigns. This is what makes it incredibly effective. Chances are, you are confused. Don't worry, just hang in there! In subsequent sections, I'll revisit this system and explain how you can use it to create and execute retargeting and remarketing campaigns.

8.3 Retargeting: A Deep Dive

As I explained earlier, retargeting brings back website visitors who left without converting. Through cookie-based tracking, you can show these potential customers relevant ads across different platforms. It's basically a gentle reminder about products or services they've already shown interest in. Let's understand its benefits, how it works, and how you can apply the L.O.O.P. framework to it.

Benefits of Retargeting

- **Higher conversion rates**: Retargeting converts three to four times better than regular ads by targeting visitors who've already shown interest.

- **Customized messaging**: Tailor ads to visitor behaviour, like offering deals to pricing-page viewers, or showing related content to blog readers.

- **Lower cost per acquisition**: Focus your budget on interested prospects instead of random audiences, thus maximizing efficiency.

- **Extended marketing reach**: Stay visible to prospects across the web, from social media to YouTube, reminding them of your products.

- **Better brand recall**: Multiple strategic reminders keep your brand memorable, so prospects think of you when ready to buy.

- **Reduced cart abandonment**: Recover 15–25 per cent of abandoned carts by reminding customers of unfinished purchases.

- **Increased return on ad spend**: Spend smarter by targeting those already interested, doubling your return on investment.

8.3.1 How Retargeting Works

Retargeting uses two key technical elements to track and reach your website visitors: tracking pixels and cookies.

- **Tracking pixels**: These are snippets of code you add to your website. Each advertising platform (like Facebook or Google) provides its own pixel code. The pixel acts like a digital sensor on your website. Here's an example of Meta pixel:

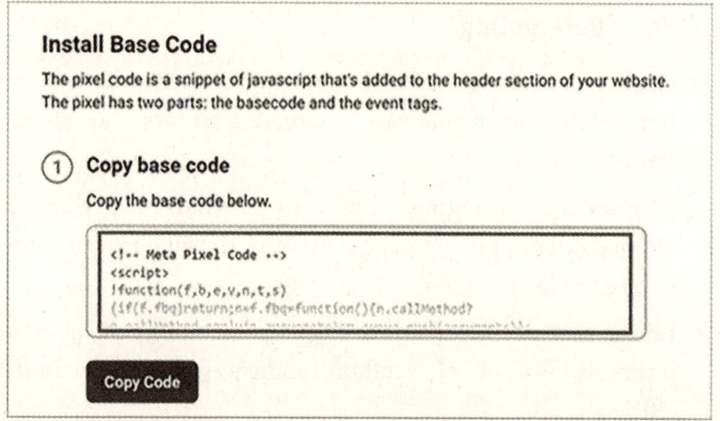

Image source: optinmonster.com, 'How Does a Retargeting Pixel Work? (3 Use Cases)', updated 20 May 2022

- **Cookies**: When someone visits your website, the pixel triggers their browser to save a cookie. This cookie is a small text file that identifies them as your website visitor. Think of pixels as the sensors that place cookies, and cookies as name tags that help identify visitors later.

Your tracking setup monitors how people interact with your website:

- o   Pages they visit
- o   Products they view
- o   Time spent on each page
- o   Items added to the cart
- o   Forms started but not completed

Now, based on the cookie data, platforms group your visitors into lists like:

- o   People who viewed specific products
- o   People who abandoned carts
- o   Visitors who spent more than two minutes on your site
- o   Those who checked the pricing pages

These groups become your retargeting audiences.

Next, when someone from your audience browses other websites or social media:

- o   Their browser cookie tells ad platforms they've visited your site
- o   The platform recognizes them as part of your audience
- o   Your ads appear on their screen

Your retargeting can run on major advertising platforms, including Google Display Network (which shows ads on millions of websites), Facebook and Instagram, LinkedIn (which is great for B2B), Twitter, and YouTube.

With your ads, you control important factors, like:

- o   How soon after the visit to start showing ads
- o   How frequently to show ads
- o   How long to keep showing ads
- o   Which ads to show to different audiences

Once set up, this system runs automatically. The pixels track visitors, cookies identify them later, and ad platforms handle the delivery. Your job? Choose the right audiences and create ads that bring them back.

8.4 Applying the L.O.O.P. Framework to Retargeting

Let's walk you through exactly how to implement each component for your retargeting campaigns.

- **Listen**

    Start with proper pixel implementation. Place your tracking pixel on every page of your website. Many founders make the mistake of adding it only to their homepage or product pages. You need complete visibility of user behaviour.

    Configure your pixel to track specific events. Beyond basic pageviews, monitor key actions like 'Add to Cart', 'Begin Checkout', or 'Contact Form Started'. Each interaction tells a story about visitor intent.

    - o   Create different audience segments based on behaviour patterns. One of our clients, a software company, discovered their most valuable audience wasn't People who abandoned carts —it was people who spent over three minutes on their features page. Your data might reveal similar unexpected insights.

- **Offer**

Match your message to the visitor's stage. Someone who viewed your pricing page shows higher purchase intent than someone who only read your blog. Your retargeting should reflect this difference.

We learned this lesson the hard way with an e-commerce client. We initially showed the same discount offer to everyone. Once we started showing product education ads to blog readers and price-match guarantees to comparison shoppers, our conversion rate doubled.

Structure your offers progressively. Start with brand awareness for recent visitors. Move to product benefits for repeat visitors. Finally, present compelling offers to those showing strong purchase intent.

- **Optimize**

Monitor performance across different segments. Track which messages resonate with specific audiences. For instance, a SaaS brand might discover that its technical blog readers convert better with feature-focused ads, while pricing page visitors respond to ROI-focused messages.

Test different ad formats. Don't limit yourself to static images. Video ads often outperform traditional banners in explaining complex products. I remember one of our B2B clients saw a 40 per cent increase in engagement after adding short demo videos to their retargeting mix.

Adjust your frequency caps based on engagement. High-intent visitors might respond well to more frequent touchpoints, while casual browsers need a lighter approach. Let the data guide these decisions.

- **Persist**

Map out your retargeting timeline. The first 24 hours after a visit are crucial, but don't stop there. I've seen conversions happen even sixty days after the initial visit, especially for high-value products.

Vary your creative content over time. People tune out repetitive ads. Rotate between different value propositions, testimonials, and offers.

Also, consider seasonal and behavioural patterns. For example, an edtech company might get better results by intensifying campaigns during admission seasons. Your business might have similar cyclical opportunities.

Note: The L.O.O.P. system isn't a one-time setup. It's an ongoing process of refinement. Your first campaign won't be perfect. But with consistent application of these principles, you'll build a retargeting machine that consistently brings visitors back and converts them into customers.

8.5 Hacks to excel at Retargeting

Over the years of managing retargeting campaigns, my team has discovered certain techniques that consistently deliver results. These aren't your typical best practices; they're specific tactics most marketers overlook.

- **The 3-3-3 Ad Rule**

Here's a visual representation of this rule:

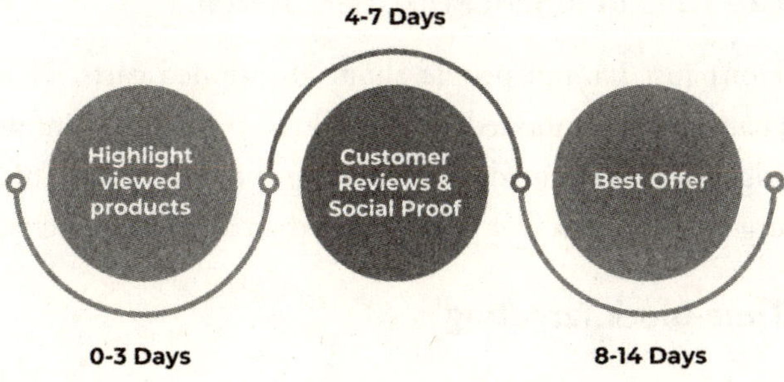

Image source: Author's illustration

Split your retargeting window into three phases: 0–3 days, 4–7 days, and 8–14 days. In each phase, show different ad types.

The first phase highlights viewed products. The second showcases customer reviews and social proof. The third presents your best offer.

This approach matches your messaging to the visitor's decision timeline. I've seen this simple adjustment increase conversion rates by a significant margin.

▪ Mobile-Desktop Cross-Device Multiplier

Most businesses run separate mobile and desktop campaigns. Instead, create segments that target users who first visited on mobile and show them desktop ads, and vice versa.

People often research on phones but purchase on computers. With our clients, we consistently see them double their conversion rate using this cross-device tactic.

- **Cart Abandonment Price Alert System**

  Don't just remind people about abandoned carts. Track price changes of abandoned items. When prices drop, immediately trigger retargeting ads, highlighting the new price. This creates urgency through real value rather than artificial scarcity.

- **Time-Block Targeting**

  Match your ad serving times to your prospects' behaviour patterns. Review your website analytics for peak engagement hours. Then create six blocks of four hours each with different budgets and bids.

  Allocate 40 per cent of your budget to your top two time blocks, 35 per cent to the next two, and 25 per cent to the lowest-performing blocks. This precision targeting often yields much better engagement rates than standard 24x7 campaigns.

- **Progressive Bid Scaling**

  Start with low bids for first-time website visitors. Double your bid for those who view multiple pages. Triple it for visitors who take high-intent actions like pricing page views or cart additions.

  This targeted bid scaling ensures you invest more in prospects showing genuine interest. This tactic can help you reduce cost per acquisition while maintaining conversion volume.

8.6 Remarketing: A Deep Dive

As explained earlier, remarketing focuses on existing customers. Through their email addresses, you can show them targeted ads across platforms like Google, Meta, and others. It's like continuing the conversation with people who already know, trust, and have experienced your brand.

Benefits of Remarketing

- **Lower acquisition costs**: Convert existing customers more cost-effectively by leveraging their prior trust and familiarity with your brand.

- **Higher customer lifetime value**: Boost revenue by encouraging repeat purchases that require less convincing and deliver long-term gains.

- **Natural purchase patterns**: Time remarketing campaigns to align with customers' buying habits, like replenishments or upgrades.

- **Precise targeting capabilities**: Use your email list for coordinated exposure across platforms, ensuring your brand stays visible to customers.

- **Smarter cross-selling**: Leverage purchase history to recommend complementary products that align naturally with customer needs.

How Remarketing Works

Remarketing starts with your customer email list. When you upload these email addresses to advertising platforms like Google Ads or Meta, something interesting happens. These platforms match your customers' email addresses with their user accounts.

For example, if your customer uses the same email for their Gmail account, Google can show them your ads while they browse YouTube or read articles on websites that display Google ads.

Each advertising platform handles remarketing differently. Google Ads reaches your customers across YouTube, Gmail, millions of websites in the Google Display Network, and Google search results. Meta connects with customers on Facebook,

Instagram, Messenger, and partner websites. LinkedIn, Twitter, and other platforms offer similar capabilities, each reaching customers within their specific ecosystems.

The email matching process protects user privacy, while enabling targeted advertising. Here's how.

- You upload your encrypted customer email list.
- Platforms compare these emails with their user database.
- When they find a match, that user becomes part of your remarketing audience.
- You never see individual user data; you only know the total size of your matched audience.

Now, your customer database opens up multiple targeting possibilities.

- All customers
- Recent customers
- High-value customers
- Product-specific customers
- Customers who haven't purchased in the last few months

Each of these segments can receive different messages and offers based on their relationship with your brand.

Once you've set up your audience segments, remarketing platforms handle the ad delivery automatically. They determine:

- When to show your ads
- Which platforms to use

- How frequently to display them
- Which version of your ad works best

The technical infrastructure makes remarketing almost hands-free once properly configured. Your job focuses on creating relevant messages for different customer segments, rather than managing the delivery mechanics.

8.7 Applying the L.O.O.P. Framework to Remarketing

You have a theoretical framework. Let's now understand how to use this L.O.O.P. system to build a remarketing campaign.

- **Listen**

  Your customer database contains gold. Export your purchase history and segment it by order value, frequency, and product categories. Look for gaps between purchases—these gaps tell you exactly when to time your ads.

  Raw purchase data also reveals product affinity. When customers consistently buy certain items together, you've found natural upsell opportunities. You'll use these insights to create targeted remarketing audiences on ad platforms.

- **Offer**

  Each advertising platform can aid different purposes in remarketing. Google Ads excel at catching customers during active shopping moments. Meta Ads work better for lifestyle and aspirational messaging. LinkedIn ads resonate when promoting business-focused upgrades.

  Match your creative to the platform. Short, punchy product ads work on Google's Display Network. Story driven content performs better on Instagram. Your email remarketing can handle longer, more detailed product explanations.

- **Optimize**

Upload your customer email lists to multiple ad platforms. Track which platform delivers the best results for different customer segments. High-value customers might engage more on LinkedIn, while frequent buyers respond better to Google Shopping ads.

Watch your audience match rates. Low match rates mean your customer emails don't align with platform user accounts. Clean your email list regularly to maintain strong match rates across platforms.

- **Persist**

Regular database updates keep your remarketing fresh. Remove customers who haven't engaged in months. Create separate lists for recent buyers versus long-term customers. Each list needs different messaging and bidding strategies.

Upload your customer lists to all major ad platforms. This creates a consistent presence wherever your customers spend time online. When they see your ads across multiple platforms, the message sinks in deeper.

8.8 Hacks to Excel at Remarketing

Most businesses upload their customer lists and hope for the best. The following advanced tactics will help you squeeze more value from your remarketing campaigns.

- **The Platform-Sync Method**

Upload your customer list to every major ad platform simultaneously. Most advertisers pick one platform, missing out opportunities on others. When Google, Meta and LinkedIn compete to show ads to the same audience, something interesting happens—your overall ad costs often drop.

Start with equal budgets across platforms. Week one might reveal LinkedIn drives sales at INR 500 per conversion while Meta costs INR 800. Adjust your bids accordingly. You'll discover certain platforms work better for different customer segments.

Here's the key though: Track platform-specific conversion costs and reallocate the budget to your best performers monthly.

▪ The Exclusion Strategy

Showing the same entry level ads to all customers wastes money and annoys loyal customers. Build your remarketing with strategic exclusions. Remove recent buyers from basic promotional campaigns for at least thirty days. Instead, show them complementary product ads or premium offerings.

But the real trick here is to create an ascending ladder of offers. Someone who just bought your basic package shouldn't see ads for it again. Show them the next level up. Keep adjusting exclusions as customers move through different purchase tiers. Your remarketing becomes a journey, not just repeated exposure.

▪ Purchase-Gap Targeting

Your customers have natural buying cycles. Open your sales data and group purchases by product type. Look for patterns in repurchase timing. Premium customers might buy every forty-five days, while regular customers take ninety days.

Create separate remarketing lists matching these intervals. The magic happens when you start ads exactly fifteen days before their expected purchase date. Your message arrives when they're already thinking about buying again. This isn't random timing but strategic anticipation of natural customer behaviour.

- **The High Match Rate Formula**

Poor match rates kill remarketing campaigns before they start. The problem here is that most customer email lists contain outdated or unusable addresses. Start by removing obvious problems: role-based emails (info@, support@), misspelled domains, and duplicates.

Here's what many miss: collect both personal and work emails from customers. Someone might use their work email to purchase but log into Facebook with their personal email. Having both doubles your chances of platform matching. This extra step in data collection often pushes match rates from 50 per cent to over 75 per cent.

- **Value-Based Bidding**

Stop treating all customers equally in your ad spend. Someone who spent INR 50,000 last year deserves a higher bid than someone who spent INR 5,000. Break your customer list into value tiers:

- Top-tier: 3x your average bid
- Mid-tier: 2x your average bid
- Regular: Standard bid

This isn't us ignoring lower-value customers. We're just investing more in proven high-value relationships. Your ad platforms will automatically optimize delivery to your most profitable segments.

8.9 A Checklist to Get Started with Retargeting and Remarketing

You've learned the concepts, strategies, and advanced tactics. Now, it's time to put everything into action. Here's your step-by-step implementation checklist:

(Both checklists assume you've already set up business accounts on major advertising platforms. Start with one platform, create a proper workflow, then expand.)

For retargeting:

- ✓ Install tracking pixels on every website page.
- ✓ Set up event tracking (page views, cart actions, form fills).
- ✓ Create audience segments based on website behaviour.
- ✓ Build custom audiences for different visitor actions.
- ✓ Design ad creatives matching visitor intent.
- ✓ Set up A/B tests to see which one performs better) for comparing different versions of ad formats.
- ✓ Configure frequency caps and delivery schedules.
- ✓ Implement the 3-3-3 rule for ad sequencing.
- ✓ Set up cross-device tracking.
- ✓ Create platform-specific budgets and bids.

For remarketing:

- ✓ Clean and organize customer email database.
- ✓ Remove invalid emails (role-based IDs, duplicates).
- ✓ Create customer segments by purchase value.
- ✓ Upload lists to advertising platforms.
- ✓ Set up value-based bidding tiers.

✓ Create platform-specific ad campaigns.

✓ Design platform-appropriate creative formats.

✓ Set up purchase-gap based targeting.

✓ Implement exclusion lists.

✓ Schedule regular list updates.

9

Connect and Converse with Email and WhatsApp

YOU'VE LIKELY BEEN THERE—SHARING YOUR NUMBER AT a retail store or café, maybe for a discount or loyalty programme. A week later, your phone buzzes endlessly with WhatsApp messages and emails, offering everything from products you don't need to updates you never asked for. You feel frustrated, ignored, and maybe even regret trusting that brand with your details.

Most of us have been on the consumer side of this story. Now, when we are asked to use WhatsApp and emails as a part of marketing strategy, we squinch up. Nobody wants to be 'the brand that spams'.

You might have collected hundreds of contacts, only to realize you don't know how to use them effectively, or worse, you are more worried about losing trust by using them poorly.

The real problem isn't just collecting customer details—it's understanding how to use them with care and strategy. How do you avoid spamming, and instead, create valuable, personalized communication? How do you ensure your messages feel welcome rather than intrusive?

With a thoughtful approach, direct marketing isn't annoying your audience; it's about building trust. Customers appreciate personalized, meaningful communication. Collecting customer data is the easy part—opt-in forms, loyalty cards, or social media giveaways—but using it effectively is where most brands falter. Instead of spamming, the focus should be on understanding the audience, segmenting them by preferences, and delivering value-driven, personalized messages.

Let's look into two real-time stories on how this can be done.

Samita runs a small fashion boutique in New Delhi. She takes her customers' phone numbers during billing. Later, she sends them WhatsApp messages about new arrivals and offers. Last month, these messages brought back 80 per cent of her previous customers.

In Bengaluru, Karan owns an education start-up. His team sends weekly emails with tips to their students' parents. These emails don't sell anything; they just help parents track their child's progress. Result? Parents now recommend these classes to other parents.

These are just two examples. From a one-person business to one as big as Mercedes-Benz (whose Turkish arm got 63 per cent of customers to take the next step toward purchase through their WhatsApp campaign), direct engagement marketing consistently delivers outstanding results—if planned and executed well, of course.[1]

Blasting WhatsApp promotional messages isn't the idea for direct engagement. Customers won't take long to label your business as spam, damaging your brand's reputation. Customers view unsolicited messages as intrusive, leading to complaints, blocking, and even account bans. This practice not only erodes trust but also alienates potential clients, reducing your credibility in the market.

In this chapter, I'll show you exactly how to use WhatsApp and email to grow your business using a proper strategy. You'll learn the F.R.I.E.N.D. formula—a system my team developed after running hundreds of campaigns for our clients. This formula guides you to write messages that sell, create campaigns that convert, and build customer relationships that last.

I'll walk you through setting up your email and WhatsApp marketing systems from scratch. You'll learn which tools to use, what messages to send, and when to send them.

Let's start with what makes WhatsApp and email marketing different from other channels.

9.1 The Magic of Direct Engagement Marketing

Direct engagement marketing builds trust and connection by communicating personally with customers, without distractions or intermediaries.

Here's what makes direct engagement so effective:

- **Zero competition for attention**: Messages go directly to customers, ensuring high visibility and response rates above 80 per cent, far surpassing mass marketing.

- **Real conversations**: Two-way communication creates deeper connections, like a jeweller I was talking to who turned one conversation into a sale worth INR 4 lakh.

- **Guaranteed reach**: Unlike social media algorithms, direct engagement ensures your message reaches everyone on your list.

- **Built-in trust**: Messages in private spaces feel personal, earning more attention and trust than public ads.

- **Cost-effective**: Ideal for start-ups, it delivers high returns at lower costs compared to paid advertising.

- **Own your data**: Direct contacts belong to you, safeguarding customer access regardless of social media changes.

I know of many businesses who lost their social media accounts and reach overnight, for one reason or another. Some of them managed to rebuild their entire customer base through direct contacts.

This method is perfect for businesses aiming to build strong, lasting customer relationships while maximizing resources.

Why Use Email and WhatsApp for Direct Engagement Marketing?

Email and WhatsApp stand out as the two most powerful channels for direct engagement marketing. Your customers already use them daily, not just for casual conversations but also for business.

Think about your own day. You check your WhatsApp messages within minutes. Important emails never go unread. Your customers behave the same way. Nearly nine out of ten people check their emails every day, and six out of ten make purchase decisions based on emails they receive.[2]

Email and WhatsApp are also not platforms of choice; they are platforms of importance. Your potential customer may or may not use any of the social media platforms they are on, but they will, by default, will have an email address and a WhatsApp account to connect with friends and family.

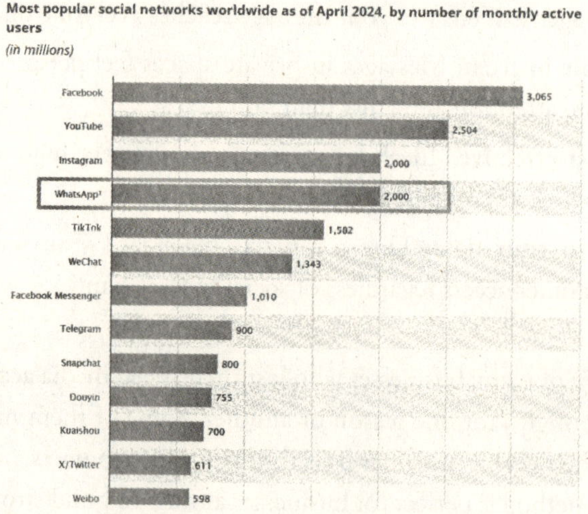

Image source: Statista.com, 2024

WhatsApp's reach in India extends beyond just urban areas. With nearly three billion active users worldwide, it's where your customers spend most of their screen time. Messages sent through WhatsApp see average open rates of 58 per cent—that's twice what you'd get on most other platforms.

I've picked these two platforms for this chapter because they work for every type of business, from small shops to large companies. You don't need big budgets or technical expertise.

Let's look at how to use these channels effectively with the F.R.I.E.N.D. formula.

9.2 The F.R.I.E.N.D. Formula

F.R.I.E.N.D. stands for Find, Reach Out, Inform, Engage, Nurture, and Develop. We developed this formula after spending years perfecting direct engagement strategies across hundreds of campaigns.

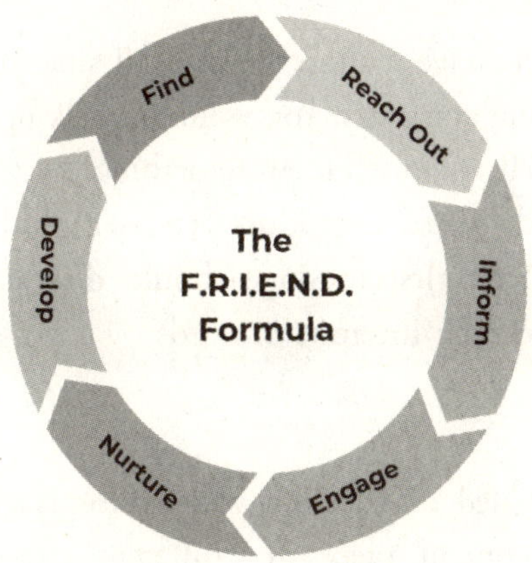

Image source: Author's illustration

One thing became obvious to me: effective direct marketing is far from sending random messages. It's a lot about building relationships, just like you do with friends.

The formula works because it mirrors how genuine friendships form—step by step, creating trust and value with each interaction.

I am sharing this formula with you because I want you to understand that successful marketing doesn't happen through shortcuts; it's built by creating a bond with your customers, turning them from strangers into loyal advocates for you and your brand.

Let me break down each element.

- **Find**

  You need the right people in your audience. I tell my clients, imagine hosting a dinner party. You wouldn't invite random strangers; you would invite people who would enjoy the food you cook. The same is true with direct marketing.

  Target customers who actually need what you sell. Look at your best customers. What do they have in common? Use these patterns to find more like them.

- **Reach Out**

  The first message matters the most. Think of it like starting a conversation at a party. You wouldn't walk up to someone and immediately try to sell them something.

  Instead, you'd introduce yourself and find common ground. Your first message should do the same. Make it relevant to their interests or needs.

- **Inform**

  Share knowledge that helps your customers. My team creates different content pieces for different stages. Someone just learning about your product needs basic information.

  Regular customers want advanced tips. Match your message to their knowledge level.

- **Engage**

  Turn monologues into dialogues. Ask questions, invite opinions, run polls—make your communication interactive. Engagement isn't about what you say, but about how your customers respond.

I've seen this first hand. One of our most successful campaigns simply asked customers, 'What's your biggest challenge right now?' The responses not only shaped future products but also made those customers feel heard and valued.

▪ Nurture

This is where most businesses lose momentum. They jump straight to the sales pitch and forget that relationships take time to grow. Nurturing means investing in the relationship.

Share exclusive tips, give them insider updates, and offer insights that help them—even if it's not directly related to what you're selling.

Make your customers feel special and valued for being part of your journey. They're far more likely to buy from you without hesitation when they feel like you're genuinely interested in their success.

▪ Develop

Once you've built that bond, it's time to grow together. Development turns a loyal customer into an advocate.

When customers succeed in using your product or service, document their journey. Celebrate their wins, share their stories, and build a community around those shared experiences.

You want your customers to see themselves in the success stories you share. When they feel like they're part of something bigger, they become brand ambassadors who spread your word. This part of the journey focuses on scaling the relationship so that it benefits everyone involved.

That's the theory behind the F.R.I.E.N.D. formula. In the subsequent sections, I'll explain exactly how you can apply this in your case. Let's start with email marketing.

9.3 Email Marketing: An In-Depth Look

What is Email Marketing?

Each email with a marketing goal serves a purpose—whether it's informing (new product launches), educating (how-to guides), selling (discounts), or building relationships (thank you notes or birthday wishes). What makes this 'marketing' is strategy: emails are sent to many people, planned to grow your business, and measured for results like opens and clicks.

Email flows, like 'welcome' or 'abandoned cart' emails, automate communication tailored to customer actions. For instance, abandoned cart emails recover 15–20 per cent of lost sales by addressing barriers like forgotten carts or incomplete info. These emails nurture trust and encourage timely conversions with well-placed reminders.

Image source: Plix.com[3]

How Does It Work?

Think of email marketing as running a store: you need a platform (your shop), a customer list, and something valuable to offer (your emails).

Start with an email marketing platform like MailChimp, Klaviyo, or ConvertKit. These tools manage sending emails, tracking performance, and handling technicalities. Next, build your email list by collecting addresses from your website, events, or sales. Quality beats quantity—100 engaged customers are better than 1,000 random addresses.

Finally, craft and send your emails. Use platform templates, personalize the content, and schedule delivery. The real magic lies in tracking: you can see exactly who opens your emails, clicks links, or takes action. This insight helps you refine your emails over time, making them even more relevant and effective.

Applying the F.R.I.E.N.D. Formula

Let me show you how each element of our F.R.I.E.N.D. formula works specifically for email marketing.

- **Find**

  Attract subscribers who genuinely need your product. Use clear sign-up forms or collect emails during purchases, emphasizing value like 'Get weekly style tips'.

- **Reach Out**

  Send a welcome email immediately with something valuable—a guide, tutorial, or discount—to set the tone and build trust.

- **Inform**

  Share useful, tailored content that makes readers feel smarter, like recipes, style tips, or product insights. Consistent value keeps them engaged.

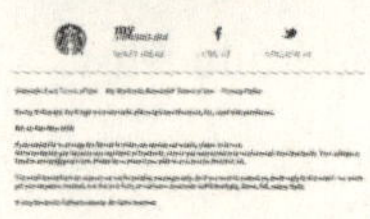

Image source:
notifyvisitors.com[4]

- **Engage**

Turn emails into conversations. Use polls, questions, or feedback requests to create emotional connections and lasting loyalty.

Here's an example of a hybrid email from Starbucks where they are first having a fun, engaging in conversation, asking their subscribers which team they belong to, followed by some hyped promotional content over their fall special PSL drinks.

- **Nurture**

Focus on consistent, helpful communication to build trust. Share newsletters, industry tips, and personal touches like festival wishes. Selling comes second.

- **Develop**

Turn subscribers into a community by sharing success stories, offering exclusives, or running interactive challenges. Build relationships that go beyond sales.

9.4 WhatsApp Marketing: An In-Depth Look

What is WhatsApp Marketing?

This uses WhatsApp Business to connect with your customers through personal messages. Unlike regular WhatsApp, the Business version gives you unique tools to manage customer conversations professionally.

Picture your neighbourhood kirana store owner who saves regular customers' numbers and messages them about fresh arrivals. Big brands like Flipkart already do this. WhatsApp marketing works the same way, but with better tools and organization. You send updates, answer questions, and solve problems—all through WhatsApp.

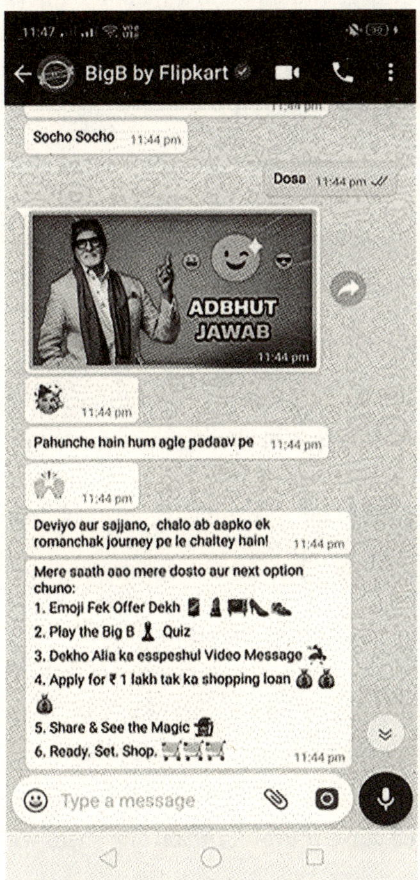

Image source: Landbot.com blog[5]

The difference from regular messaging is that you get business-specific features: a proper business profile with your shop's timings and location, quick-reply templates for common questions, labels to organize different types of customers, and automated messages when you're busy.

How Does It Work?

WhatsApp marketing needs three key elements: WhatsApp Business app (or API), a message strategy, and a system to manage conversations. Let's start with the tools.

- **WhatsApp Business App**

  It's perfect if you're just starting out. It's free and works like regular WhatsApp. Download it from the Play Store or App Store. You'll need a separate phone number from your personal WhatsApp. Most businesses use a new SIM card just for this.

- **WhatsApp Business API**

  This is for more extensive operations. It lets you connect WhatsApp to your business software, handle messages from multiple team members, and send bulk updates. Popular platforms like Intercom and Gupshup help set this up. The cost varies based on your use case.

The actual working process has three parts:

1. **Setup**: Create a business profile with hours, location, and product photos to establish credibility.
2. **Messaging**: Use broadcast lists for updates and chats for personal conversations, organizing them with labels.
3. **Tracking**: Monitor stats like sent, delivered, and read messages to refine your approach.

Think of it like running a physical store. Your profile is your storefront, messages are your conversations with customers, and analytics help you serve them better.

Applying the F.R.I.E.N.D. Formula

Let me show you how to adapt our formula specifically for WhatsApp marketing.

- **Find**

  Collect phone numbers ethically by adding WhatsApp buttons to your site, QR codes in store, or 'Message us on WhatsApp' on packaging. Always ask for permission: 'Can I send you updates on WhatsApp?'

- **Reach Out**

  Your first message should set clear expectations. Welcome them warmly but professionally: 'Thanks for connecting! We'll send weekly updates every Monday. Reply "stop" anytime to unsubscribe.'

Image source: Store Next Door welcome message from Peppercloud.com blog[6]

- **Inform**

  Share quick, visual updates like today's specials, styling tips, or study hacks. Keep messages short and engaging—long paragraphs don't work on WhatsApp.

- **Engage**

  Make interactions personal. Use names, ask for feedback, or share behind-the-scenes content. Reply promptly to messages to build trust and stronger relationships.

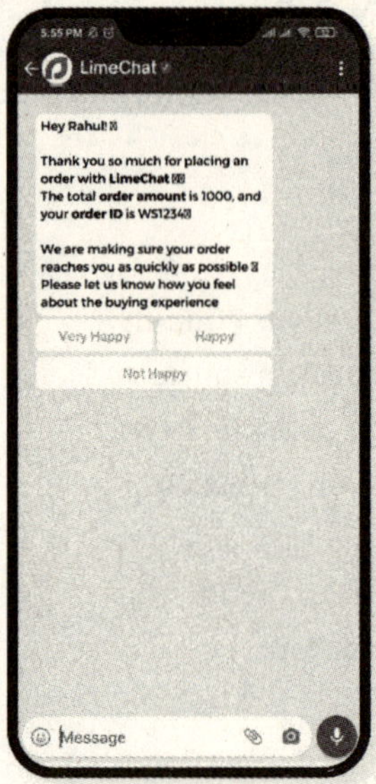

Image source: Limechat.AI[7]

- **Nurture**

  Stick to a consistent rhythm—weekly tips, monthly offers, or regular updates. Use broadcast messages for big announcements and status updates for quick news. Always respect WhatsApp's intimacy.

- **Develop**

  Turn loyal customers into advocates by creating VIP groups, sharing exclusive previews, or asking for feedback. Thoughtful communication can turn WhatsApp into a powerful community building tool.

9.5 A Quick Checklist to Get Started

Here's your step-by-step action plan to launch your direct engagement marketing. Follow these steps in order—each builds on the previous one and helps you create a solid foundation.

- ✓ Set up WhatsApp Business app with a dedicated business number.
- ✓ Choose an email marketing platform (MailChimp/Zoho for beginners).
- ✓ Create your business profile on both platforms with complete details.
- ✓ Build your first message template bank with welcome messages.
- ✓ Set up a simple lead capture form on your website for email collection.
- ✓ Create a QR code for easy WhatsApp contact addition.
- ✓ Write your welcome message sequence for both channels.
- ✓ Set up basic automation for welcome messages.
- ✓ Create your first customer segments (new, active, inactive).
- ✓ Plan your first month of content using the F.R.I.E.N.D. formula.
- ✓ Test all messages on different devices before sending.
- ✓ Set up a basic tracking system (opens, clicks, responses).
- ✓ Create response templates for common customer queries.
- ✓ Schedule your first broadcast message.
- ✓ Monitor responses for the first week.
- ✓ Adjust your approach based on customer engagement.

10

From Outreach to Impact: Influencer Marketing Done Right

'EVERYONE'S WATCHING, BUT ARE THEY REALLY BUYING?'[1] You see their big follower numbers, the endless likes and comments, and you think, 'This has to work—it's how everyone's growing their brand.' So, you go for it. You spend hours picking the right influencers, excited about their audience size, and waiting for that big moment when your product/service takes off. But when the posts go live, nothing really happens. The likes come in, but the sales don't. The comments are all generic, and your brand barely gets mentioned.

It hits hard, and you start questioning everything. Did you pick the wrong influencer? Or worse—does influencer marketing even work? You can't help but feel frustrated and let down. It's not just about the money you spent! It makes you wonder: Is this all just hype? Am I doing something wrong? Or is there a better way to actually connect with the people who matter to my business?

On the other hand, you hear stories like these.

Priti Goenka had a boutique shop in a mall in Pune, selling makeup items. She wanted to expand her reach to college-going girls looking for trendy, affordable products, but lacked the budget for traditional advertising.

To solve this, she partnered with micro-influencers on Instagram—local students who were passionate about makeup and had strong connections with her target audience. Priti provided them with her products, and they shared their experiences online.

Within just a few weeks, Priti saw a 30 per cent increase in sales, and many customers mentioned discovering her store through these Instagram posts.

The same story repeats for Rajen Khati, who runs a local handmade jewellery brand in Gangtok and faced a similar challenge. He wanted to increase both online orders and in-store visits. He collaborated with local fashion content creators who shared his jewellery through their Instagram posts. Soon enough, Rajen saw a nearly 82 per cent increase in inquiries, and a notable rise in both online and in-store purchases.

There are stories after stories of small businesses leveraging influencers to increase their sales and build strong brand recognition.

So, the million-dollar question is: Which part of the game are you missing?

One of the biggest mistakes in influencer marketing is focusing on follower count while ignoring engagement. Sure, an influencer might have hundreds of thousands of followers, but how many are actually liking, commenting, or sharing their posts? If their audience isn't engaging, what are you really paying for? Are you reaching people who care, or just adding to the noise? High numbers look good, but without trust and interaction, your message won't stick.

Another common misstep is not aligning the influencer's values with your brand's ethos. For example, imagine a fitness brand promoting weight-loss products partnering with a lifestyle influencer who advocates for body positivity and self-acceptance. While the influencer might have a loyal following, their audience could view the collaboration as tone-deaf or even offensive. This mismatch not only risks alienating the influencer's followers, but also damages your brand's reputation.

In this chapter, I'll cover how to use influencer marketing effectively. I'll talk about the M.A.T.C.H. rule you'll use to find the right influencers for your business goals, and even give you some actionable tips that my team has used when working with some of the biggest brands on behalf of our clients.

By the end, you'll know how to leverage influencers' reach to drive higher sales and scale your business.

Influencers connect with their followers through engaging content, building trust and genuine relationships. You can tap into this trust to promote your brand by leveraging their platforms, which often have highly engaged audiences. These influencers use their platforms—like Instagram, YouTube, TikTok, and blogs—to endorse products or services authentically.

Different Types of Influencers

Influencers come in different forms and each type serves a unique purpose. Knowing when to use each can help you make the right choice for your brand.

- **Nano Influencers (1,000–10,000 followers)**

  High engagement rates make them perfect for start-ups, niche products, or local outreach on a budget. Their personal recommendations build trust.

- **Micro Influencers (10,000–100,000 followers)**

  Great for reaching specific communities while maintaining strong engagement and credibility. They're ideal for driving conversions.

- **Macro Influencers (100,000–1 million followers)**

  Best for wide visibility and awareness campaigns. While engagement is lower, they reach large audiences quickly.

10.2 The M.A.T.C.H. Rule: Find the Right Influencers for Your Brand

You can pay the biggest influencers the most money, but if they don't align with key principles of effective influencer marketing, your ROI will be low.

To solve this, my team and I developed the M.A.T.C.H. rule—a framework we use for all our clients' influencer marketing campaigns. It helps us find the right influencers and ensure that each partnership maximizes results for our clients.

Let's break it down.

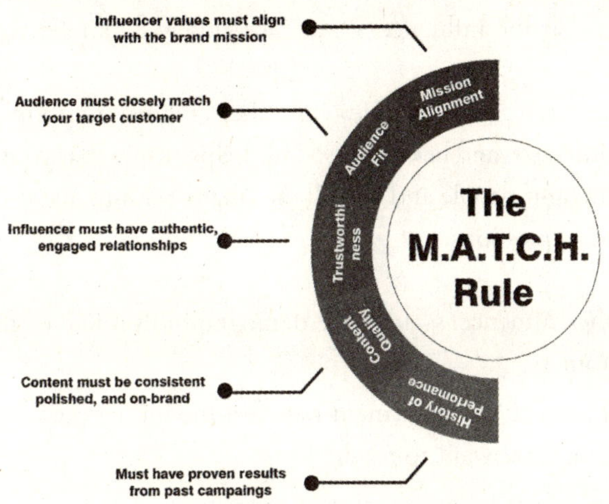

Image source: Author's illustration

M: Mission Alignment

This is the first step to building a successful influencer partnership. The influencer's values, content, and passion must align with your brand's mission.

You want someone who genuinely believes in your product and shares a similar vision. This creates authenticity, which is key to building trust with the audience. Here are some questions you should ask when matching with an influencer:

- Are the influencer's passions similar to those of my brand?
- Does their content support the kind of values my brand promotes?
- Do they talk about topics that match my brand's purpose?
- Would their followers connect naturally with my brand's mission?
- Are they aligned with my brand's messaging and values?

A: Audience Fit

Audience fit is more than just looking at follower numbers; you need to make sure that the influencer's audience closely resembles your target customer.

Analyse their demographics: are they aligned in terms of age, location, interests, and behaviours? This helps ensure that your message reaches the right people and actually resonates with them.

Ask these questions:

- Is the influencer's audience demographic similar to my target customer?
- Is there a clear engagement between the influencer and the type of people we want to reach?
- Would their followers value our product?

T: Trustworthiness

An influencer might have lots of followers, but if there's no genuine relationship with their audience, it won't work. You need to evaluate their authenticity and credibility.

Look at how followers engage with them. Ask:

- Do followers leave meaningful comments, showing genuine interest?

- Has the influencer been consistent in their messaging?
- Does the influencer respond to their followers in a meaningful way?

Trustworthy influencers often share their honest opinions, not just paid promotions, which plays a big role in building a lasting relationship with them and improving your ROI in the long-term.

C: Content Quality

Content quality is about how well the influencer's style fits your brand. Their posts need to be polished, authentic, and consistent. They should match your brand's aesthetics and tone.

The influencer also needs a storytelling approach that resonates with your brand's personality—this helps convey your message effectively.

Here are a few questions to answer when analysing influencers' content:

- Is their content polished and professional?
- Does their style align with your brand's aesthetics?
- Do they create content that fits well with your brand's tone?

H: History of Performance

History of performance gives you insight into how an influencer's past campaigns have fared. It's not just about their reach but also about whether they've driven meaningful engagement and actions.

Look at their past metrics—did they help brands boost sales, increase engagement, or change customer sentiment? Performance history helps predict future success. Ask:

- How have their previous campaigns performed?
- What are their engagement rates like?
- Did their past partnerships lead to measurable results for other brands?

- Have they worked with similar brands successfully in the past?

The M.A.T.C.H. framework ensures every influencer you partner with is a good fit for your brand in all the critical areas.

When you use M.A.T.C.H., you align missions, audiences, and trust, while ensuring quality content and evaluating performance history—all of which combine to create a more effective influencer campaign.

10.3 How to Build Relationships, Not Just Transactions

Once you've used the M.A.T.C.H. rule to find the right influencers, focus on building meaningful relationships, not just treating partnerships as transactions. This is important.

One-off transactions limit your campaign's potential. Influencers are not just media channels; they are individuals with loyal audiences. When you build real relationships, influencers become passionate about your brand, which means genuine content and better results.

Influencers who feel valued will work harder for you. They'll share content that goes beyond expectations, provide honest endorsements, and support your brand consistently. Building these strong connections turns influencers into advocates who go the extra mile.

Let's look into a real-life brand example, that of U.S. shoe and clothing retailer Zappos.

The company has restructured its influencer marketing strategy to prioritize authenticity and inclusivity. Instead of collaborating with top-tier influencers and celebrities, the company now focuses on engaging everyday individuals who genuinely resonate with their brand values. For instance, in early 2024, Zappos launched the 'Start Where You Are' campaign, featuring real-life runners from diverse backgrounds, such as a new mother, a U.S. Marine Corps veteran, a women's fitness instructor, and a podcast host. This shift underscores Zappos' commitment to inclusivity and connecting with a broader audience by highlighting relatable stories and experiences.[2]

Image source: FitandFemale.net/partnerships

In my experience, how you build this relationship varies based on the influencer's style and the context of your campaign. However, there are some fundamental steps that my team follows to create lasting, impactful connections.

1. Personalize outreach by referencing their specific content and treating each influencer as unique.

2. Offer value beyond money with exclusive access, co-creation opportunities, or early samples.

3. Maintain open communication through regular check-ins and by incorporating their feedback.

4. Trust influencers' creative freedom to craft genuine, relatable content for their audience.

5. Focus on long-term collaborations to build consistent, authentic connections and loyalty.

Building relationships takes time, but it's worth it. From what I have seen time and again for our clients, when influencers feel valued, they become loyal advocates who genuinely want to promote your brand. This authenticity drives real engagement and successful campaigns.

10.4 Planning and Executing Campaigns: Seven-Step Process

There can be many small and big steps involved in planning and executing an influencer marketing campaign. The size and scope of these steps depend on the brand you're working with. For example, a big fashion brand will experience more friction due to complex decision-making processes and approvals, while a showroom in UB City Mall in Bengaluru might have a much quicker planning and execution cycle.

In general, here are the steps my team follows to create effective and well-executed influencer campaigns. Let's dive into each of them.

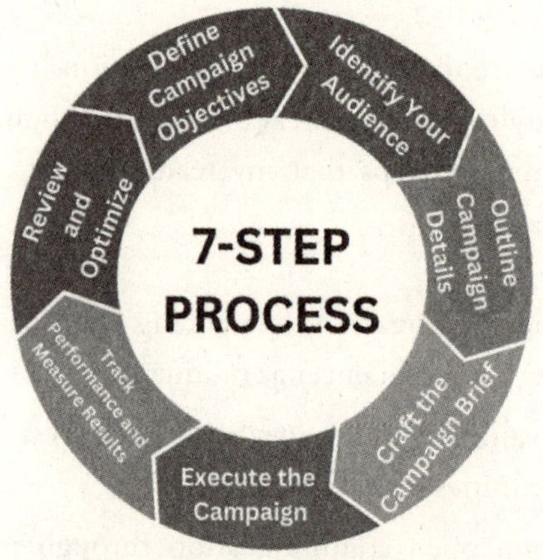

Image source: Author's illustration

Step 1: Define Campaign Objectives

You need to define your campaign objectives before doing anything else. This means understanding what you want to achieve—whether it's brand awareness, increased sales, or community engagement.

So, what do you want from this campaign? Increased sales? Brand visibility? New leads? Be specific. Once the goal is clear, identify metrics. If you want more brand awareness, measure impressions and reach. If it's about sales, track conversions.

Step 2: Identify Your Audience

Knowing who you want to reach is essential. A clear understanding of your target audience will guide you in selecting the right influencers and crafting the right message.

Start by creating audience personas—define key details like age, location, interests, and online behaviour. Picture your ideal customer.

Next, match your audience with influencer demographics. Your influencer's audience should mirror your target market, so look at their demographics, interests, and engagement styles.

Finally, validate the audience fit. Don't just take demographics at face value. Validate the fit through tools and engagement analysis.

Step 3: Outline Campaign Details

Details are everything. You need to lay down a comprehensive plan that includes every aspect of the campaign. Decide on content types—whether influencers will do unboxings, reviews, tutorials, or behind-the-scenes content.

Choose platforms based on where your audience spends their time, such as Instagram, YouTube, or TikTok (outside India).

Lastly, create a timeline that includes when posts should go live, feedback loops, and deadlines for deliverables.

Step 4: Craft the Campaign Brief

A good brief is the backbone of a successful campaign. It ensures that influencers have all the context they need to deliver content that aligns with your brand. Include brand guidelines that explain your mission, tone, and visual aesthetics.

Be clear on deliverables, including the number of posts, stories, hashtags to use, and key messages. But remember, while you want to set expectations, provide room for influencers to use their creativity.

Step 5: Execute the Campaign

This is where everything comes together. Coordinate posting schedules to make sure all content goes live as planned. Use scheduling tools if necessary.

Be available to assist influencers with any questions or issues that might arise during execution. Also, monitor activity in real time to see how audiences are engaging with the posts.

Step 6: Track Performance and Measure Results

Once the campaign is live, tracking its performance is key to understanding its impact. Track engagement metrics like likes, comments, shares, and overall engagement to gauge resonance.

Use promo codes or tracking links to measure sales or sign-ups driven by the campaign.

Additionally, look at sentiment analysis to understand how people are responding to the campaign. Is the tone positive? Are there recurring questions or themes?

Step 7: Review and Optimize

After the campaign ends, take time to analyse what worked and what didn't. Identify specific strategies that led to the most engagement and positive feedback. Recognize which influencers and content formats performed the best, and consider how to replicate those aspects in the future.

Look closely at areas where there could have been improvements, whether it's adjusting the timing of posts, refining content quality, or choosing better influencer fits.

Document all learnings in detail and take actionable notes on insights gained for future campaigns to ensure continuous improvement.

10.5 How to Measure Success

Measuring the success of an influencer marketing campaign helps you know what worked, what didn't, and how you can refine your strategy for future campaigns. Let's look at the key ways to measure success, broken down into clear steps.

➢ Engagement Metrics

Engagement metrics show how well your content resonates with the audience. Measure likes, comments, shares, and saves to see if people are interacting. High engagement means the content is connecting. On an average engagement rate of 2.5–5 per cent is considered to be very healthy.

➢ Reach and Impressions

Reach is the number of unique users who see your content, while impressions count the total views. These metrics show visibility and whether users are seeing your content multiple times.

➢ Conversion Tracking

Conversions directly impact your business goals, like purchases or sign-ups. Measure conversions using promo codes, unique links, or landing page traffic to determine if the campaign led to desired actions.

➢ Brand Mentions and Awareness

Brand mentions show how well your campaign spreads awareness. Track mentions, hashtags, and tags to determine if people are discussing your brand organically.

➢ Return on Investment

This shows if the campaign was worth the cost. Compare campaign expenses to revenue generated to evaluate profitability and consider brand value gains like increased credibility.

What you measure and which metrics you track will often depend on your campaign's specific goals. During the planning phase, we set and define these metrics clearly—establishing which metrics to measure, how exactly to measure them, and the specific numbers we aim to achieve.

My team always emphasizes breaking down metrics based on these goals to understand how each campaign performed. This approach helps us see what worked and where adjustments can be made to improve future outcomes.

10.6 Checklist to Get Started

- ✓ Define your campaign goals to determine what you want to achieve.
- ✓ Identify your target audience and create detailed audience personas.

✓ Research influencer types like nano, micro, macro, or niche to match your goals.

✓ Set your budget and break it down by influencer type or tier.

✓ Use the M.A.T.C.H. rule to find influencers that align with your brand.

✓ Research and shortlist influencers using tools or manual analysis.

✓ Reach out with personalized messages explaining why they fit your campaign.

✓ Discuss compensation clearly, including monetary and product exchange options.

✓ Craft a campaign brief with guidelines, goals, and messaging points.

✓ Establish a timeline with posting schedules and deadlines for content.

✓ Decide on content types that best suit your audience and brand.

✓ Set clear metrics to measure the success of the campaign.

✓ Track performance in real time to make necessary adjustments.

✓ Analyse post-campaign results to document insights for the future.

11

Building Your Digital PR Engine: A Foolproof System

IN EARLY 2024, I BUMPED INTO RAHUL JAIN, MY MBA BUDDY, who is running an edtech platform in Hyderabad. 'Our product helps hundreds of students score better in competitive exams. But nobody knows we exist,' he told me. His team had great case studies, strong testimonials, and impressive data. Yet, they struggled to get any media attention.

Knowing about my background, he requested I review their PR strategy; specifically, digital PR strategy. After hearing him in detail, I proposed a small tweak in the existing game plan—instead of pushing generic press releases, ask your team to share real student success stories. Next, start publishing exam preparation insights based on the platform's data. And finally, reach out to education journalists and bloggers who extensively cover exam trends.

Within four months, Rahul's platform was featured in five major education publications; their website traffic tripled.

Compare this with Priya's handmade skincare brand in Pune. She wanted to compete with big beauty companies but had a limited marketing budget. Her solution? She built relationships with micro-influencers and beauty bloggers. She invited them to see how she sourced ingredients from local farmers. She shared her journey of creating natural formulations in her home kitchen.

The results surprised everyone. Beauty magazines started covering her brand's farm-to-face approach. Local businesses reached out for partnerships. Her products now sell in premium stores across Maharashtra.

These stories show how strategic digital PR helps businesses gain visibility and credibility. Whether you're a tech start-up seeking media coverage or a small business building a local presence, targeted PR efforts amplify your message to the right audience.

In this chapter, I'll show you how to build your own digital PR engine—a system to get meaningful media coverage and build lasting industry relationships. You'll learn:

- How to create stories journalists want to cover.
- A framework to plan and execute PR campaigns that deliver results.
- The C.L.E.A.R. system we use to help businesses stand out in crowded markets.

Let's start with understanding what effective digital PR looks like today.

Understanding Digital PR

Digital PR focuses on managing how your business is represented and perceived online. Unlike traditional PR, which prioritizes offline channels such as newspapers and television, digital PR targets the spaces where your audience is most active—online on platforms like websites, news portals, blogs, social media, and search engines.

At its heart, digital PR builds trust and drives visibility. It involves creating impactful stories about your brand and sharing them through the right digital channels. This might include pitching articles to industry publications, collaborating with influencers to expand your reach, or addressing customer feedback directly on platforms like Google and Yelp.

Digital PR isn't a one-time campaign; it's an ongoing conversation with your customers, industry peers, and the broader online community. Whether your goal is to strengthen your reputation, improve search rankings, or increase brand awareness, digital PR gives you the capabilities to make that happen.

Why Is It Important?

Picture this: Your competitor's product has more bugs than yours. Their customer service isn't great. Their prices are higher. Yet, they're growing faster than you. Why?

People trust them more. Their online presence makes them look more credible than your business.

This happens more often than you'd think. I see it with my clients all the time—solid products getting overlooked because they haven't built the right online presence.

Here's why digital PR matters for your business:

- Google search results shape first impressions of your brand before anyone visits your website.

- Positive media mentions give you an edge when customers compare you with competitors.

- Industry recognition helps you charge premium prices for your products or services.

- Positive coverage brings inbound partnership opportunities from other businesses.

- Digital PR builds credibility that makes sales conversations easier.

- Online reputation directly impacts your customer acquisition costs.

- Local PR helps you dominate your geographical market against bigger competitors.
- A strong online presence attracts better talent; people want to work for well-known companies.

11.1 How to Plan and Execute a Digital PR Strategy

Digital PR needs clear goals and the right tools. So, what are you trying to achieve? Do you want to:

- Fix a damaged reputation?
- Build credibility in your industry?
- Attract customers in your local area?
- Position yourself as a thought leader?
- Create trust for your new product?

I always tell my clients: focus on one main goal. Your PR strategy changes based on what you want to achieve.

Next, you need to clearly understand what you need, in order to plan and execute a digital PR strategy to achieve the goals you've defined. Here's what an essential toolkit might look like:

- A monitoring system to track mentions of your business online.
- A list of relevant journalists and influencers in your industry.
- Strong company profiles on key platforms (Google Business, LinkedIn).
- A simple content calendar for sharing company updates.
- Email templates for reaching out to media contacts.
- A crisis communication plan.

Many founders skip the planning phase. They jump straight into sending press releases or posting on social media. That's precisely what happened with one of our clients—a software company in Hyderabad. They spent six months pushing out content randomly. Zero results.

The same company later used our C.L.E.A.R. system. This time, they planned everything. They knew exactly who they wanted to reach. They built relationships with tech journalists before pitching stories. The results? Four major media features in three months.

The C.L.E.A.R. system breaks down digital PR into simple, manageable steps. In the next section, I'll share this system with you. It helps you:

- Create the right message for your audience.
- Pick the best channels to reach them.
- Build genuine relationships with media contacts.
- Measure what's working (and fix what isn't).

11.2 The C.L.E.A.R. System

The C.L.E.A.R. system is a structured approach to planning and executing digital PR campaigns that deliver results. It simplifies the process by breaking it into five actionable steps:

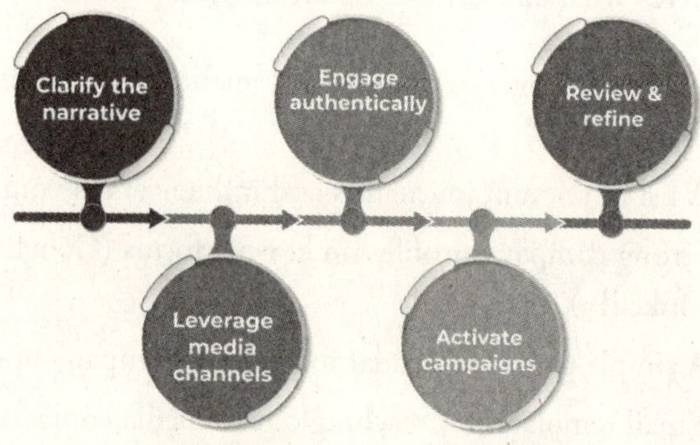

The C.L.E.A.R. System

Image source: Author's illustration

This system works because it focuses on strategy, execution, and iteration, addressing common challenges such as unclear messaging, wasted efforts on the wrong platforms, and ineffective follow-up.

Let's break it down step by step.

(i) Clarify the Narrative

Your narrative is the foundation of your digital PR efforts. It determines how your audience perceives your brand and whether they'll connect with it emotionally.

A strong narrative is more than a catchy slogan; it's the underlying story that conveys your purpose, values, and what sets you apart from competitors.

This narrative acts as the lens through which all your PR activities are crafted. It's what makes your message resonate with journalists, influencers, and, most importantly, your audience. Without clarity here, your PR efforts risk becoming scattered and ineffective.

(ii) Leverage Media Channels

A compelling message alone isn't enough; it needs to reach the right people through platforms they trust and engage with regularly. Media channels are the bridges between your story and your audience.

From industry-specific blogs to mainstream news outlets, each channel plays a role in amplifying your narrative. Choosing the wrong platforms wastes time and effort, while selecting the right ones maximizes your impact.

Knowing where your audience is most active ensures your message isn't just seen but actively absorbed, helping to build credibility and drive engagement.

(iii) Engage Authentically

PR is not just about getting coverage; it's a lot about building relationships that stand the test of time. Authentic engagement focuses on genuine human connections with media professionals, influencers, and your audience.

People are more likely to listen when they feel valued and understood, so your interactions should show that you're invested in creating mutual value.

Remember, authenticity doesn't just build trust; it fosters loyalty, making those who interact with your brand more likely to advocate for it in the future.

(iv) Activate Campaigns

Planning and executing campaigns is where your strategy becomes actionable and results start to materialize. Each campaign is an opportunity to align your narrative with a specific goal, whether it's launching a product, improving your reputation, or increasing visibility.

Well-activated campaigns ensure that all your efforts—from media outreach to content creation—are working together cohesively to create measurable impact. Without a well-thought-out campaign structure, PR efforts can lack the focus and intensity needed to produce tangible outcomes.

A good campaign captures attention, yes. But, at the same time, it also motivates your audience to act, whether that's through clicks, shares, or purchases.

(v) Review and Refine

Digital PR is not a one-and-done activity. The market is always evolving, and your strategy needs to adapt alongside it. Reviewing your efforts regularly allows you to understand what's working, and identify areas for improvement.

It's truly a process of learning and optimization, ensuring that each campaign builds on the successes and lessons of the previous one.

This step is about fine-tuning your approach based on real-world data, ensuring your efforts stay relevant and effective over time. Skipping this step can lead to stagnation or repeating mistakes, so reviewing and refining ensures your PR remains a dynamic, living process.

11.3 Digital PR Tactics That Actually Work

These tactics tackle specific challenges, boost visibility, and establish your brand's credibility. Each focuses on practical, result-oriented strategies—whether it's solving precise customer problems, creating content that journalists want to feature, or turning emerging trends into opportunities. They provide actionable steps to strengthen your brand's reputation and make a lasting impact online.

11.3.1 Micro-Moment PR

Focus on solving specific, often-overlooked customer challenges with highly targeted campaigns. Identify pain points using tools like Google Trends or surveys and create messages that resonate.

Example: Zomato's meal-time notifications remind users of favourite dishes and offer timely discounts, driving frequent orders.

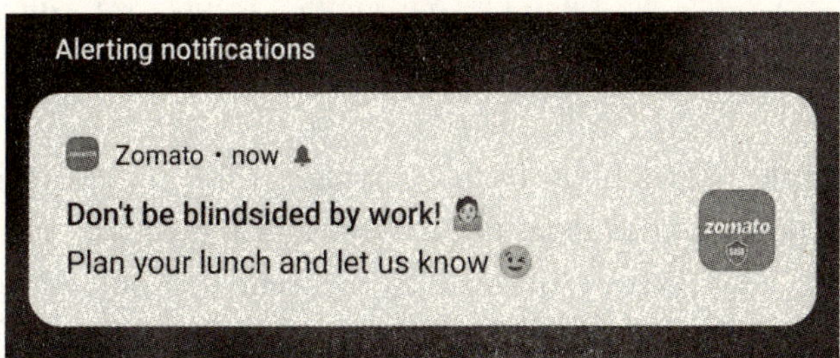

Image source: Medium.com/@gargchhavi76[1]

11.3.2 Press Release

Modern press releases include videos, infographics, and ready-to-use quotes to appeal to journalists and digital audiences. Host these assets on a sharable link to simplify access.

Example: Licious gained visibility by celebrating its 'Farm to Fork Promise' with a multimedia press release featuring videos, infographics, and customer testimonials, earning mentions in major outlets like Inc42 and Mint.

Image source: Inc42.com[2]

11.3.3 The 'Local Hero' Approach

Build goodwill by partnering with local causes or nonprofits that align with your brand's values. Highlight tangible results (like meals donated or workshops conducted) with visuals and stories.

Example: Paper Boat blends nostalgia with cultural pride by reintroducing traditional Indian beverages and collaborating with artists. This strategy drove a 16 per cent year-on-year revenue growth and reduced losses by 48 per cent in FY24.[3] Storyboard 18

Image source: Shikhar Gupta's LinkedIn post[4]

11.3.4 Crisis Prevention Monitoring

Proactively monitor mentions and complaints using tools like Brand24 or Google Alerts. Prepare response templates and act quickly to prevent escalation.

Example: In 2013, Buffer swiftly handled a security breach by pausing activity, issuing clear updates, and resolving the issue transparently. This approach not only mitigated fallout but also reinforced user trust.[5]

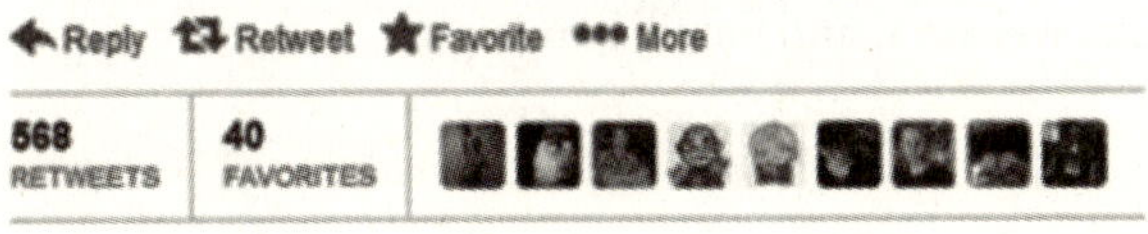

Image source: Search Engine Watch[6]

11.3.5 Trend Hijacking

Spot emerging trends early with tools like BuzzSumo and Google Trends. Craft a unique, data-backed perspective and pitch it before the trend fades.

Example: Boondh, a sustainable period care brand, aligned its campaigns with World Environment Day and plastic waste reduction, using hashtags like #SustainablePeriod to increase visibility and drive sales.

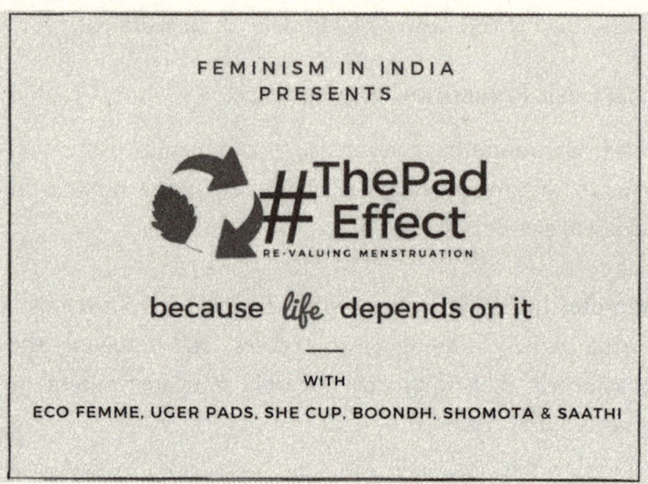

Image source: FeminisminIndia.com[7]

11.3.6 Social Proof Stacking

Build credibility by showcasing customer reviews, media mentions, awards, and influencer endorsements. Repurpose these across social media, websites, and email campaigns.

Example: BoAt became India's number one wearables brand by combining quality products with influencer partnerships and strong social proof, solidifying its market dominance.

Image source: Winnerbrands.in[8]

11.3.7 Create Data-Driven Reports

Data-driven reports provide journalists with exclusive insights. Conduct surveys or analyse internal data, and package findings into visually appealing, actionable reports.

Example: Sula Vineyards leveraged data on wine consumption trends in tier-2 and tier-3 cities to adjust its strategy, leading to growth and enhanced brand visibility through campaigns like #SulaWineAwareness.

Image source: Reuters[9]

11.4 A Quick Checklist to Get Started with Digital PR

A strong digital PR strategy will help you increase visibility, build trust and meaningful connections with your audience, while also managing your communications effectively when a crisis hits. Follow this checklist to get started:

- ✓ Define a single PR goal, such as building credibility or fixing your reputation.

- ✓ Write a one-sentence brand narrative that captures your purpose and uniqueness.

- ✓ Audit all online profiles for accuracy and professionalism.

- ✓ Use Google Analytics or other tools to identify where your target audience consumes content.

- ✓ Build a media list of journalists and influencers using BuzzSumo or Hunter.io.

- ✓ Set up Google Alerts, Brand24, or Mention to track brand mentions and industry-specific keywords.

- ✓ Create customizable email templates for pitches, review requests, and influencer collaborations.
- ✓ Gather testimonials, awards, and certifications into a shareable social proof database.
- ✓ Plan PR activities for the next thirty days with a simple content calendar.
- ✓ Identify a specific customer pain point and launch a micro-moment campaign to address it.
- ✓ Develop a press release template with multimedia elements like videos and infographics.
- ✓ Find a niche publication or local outlet and pitch a story tailored to their audience.
- ✓ Partner with a non-profit or local organization and pitch the story to community media.
- ✓ Use Google Forms or Typeform to conduct a small survey for a data-driven PR report.
- ✓ Draft a crisis communication plan with pre-approved responses for common issues.

12

Marketplace Mastery: Ins and Outs of Amazon, Flipkart, and More

AT THE OUTSET, LET US READ THE STORY OF MR BAGARIA from Jaipur in his own words.

'I started my journey in the handloom business in Jaipur with a passion for preserving my family's legacy. Each piece we crafted here reflected years of tradition and hard work. But lately, I've watched our sales decline. Rising rents and tough competition from larger, newer stores have made it hard to keep up. I fear that with this new way of doing business, I might not be able to continue this legacy that has been a part of my family for generations.

The thought of closing the doors weighs heavily on me, not just because of the financial struggles, but because I worry about disappointing my family and the loyal customers who have supported us. Like many small business owners, I feel the pressure to adapt and find new ways to survive in a changing market. The uncertainty is overwhelming, I don't know where to begin and I find myself at the crossroads of possibly letting go of something I hold so dear.'

Does this sound familiar?

Many offline sellers face similar challenges: geographical limitations, high operational costs, and difficulty in reaching new customers. These problems are pushing businesses to explore online marketplaces as a solution.

Do You Sell Your Products Online?

Empirical evidence and studies make it extremely apparent that you need to take your physical products to online marketplaces, no matter what you sell—pens, watches, candies, handmade jewellery, perfumes, grocery items, pastries, electrical equipment, clothing, mobile phones, or anything and everything else.

Online marketplaces can transform a business, like they did for Pratik Doshi, who became a millionaire selling umbrellas.

In 2014, Pratik started a venture—Cheeky Chunk—that sold designer umbrellas. He used marketplaces like Amazon, Flipkart, and Snapdeal. The product received positive responses from the public, and soon started recording big numbers in sales. So much so that Pratik has become one of Amazon India's most prominent success stories.[1] But he's not alone.

There are millions of businesses in India that sell online through top marketplaces. In 2023 alone, three lakh new sellers joined Amazon.[2] In the same year, an estimated 2.5 crore Indians shopped online. This number is expected to reach 4.25 crore by 2027.

However, all said and done, success isn't a default for all sellers; it requires a strategic approach. Through my years of experience helping local businesses strategically establish and expand their stores online, I've developed a framework called the Visibility Pyramid. This framework outlines the key elements that contribute to marketplace success:

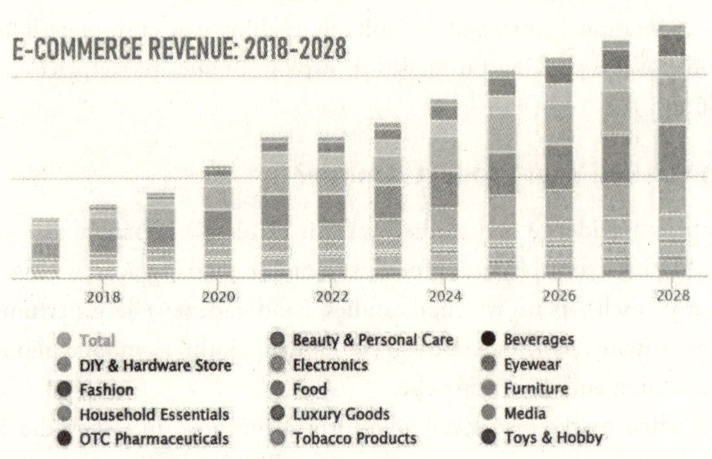

Image source: Statista.com[3]

- Listing your products properly.

- Effective marketplace SEO tactics.

- Leveraging customer reviews and ratings.

- Strategic use of platform advertising tools.

- Building brand authority over time.

Each of these elements helps increase your visibility, drive sales, and establish your brand on online marketplaces.

In this chapter, I'll help you understand what works on Indian marketplaces, the Visibility Pyramid, and sales acceleration tactics my team has used to help small and medium-sized businesses (SMBs) crack seven-figure monthly sales online. But first, let's start with the basics.

12.1 Understanding the Basics

What are online marketplaces?

Online marketplaces are websites or apps where multiple sellers list and sell products. In India, popular examples include Flipkart, Amazon India, Meesho and more. These platforms handle product listings, payments, and often, shipping. They earn through commissions on sales, and sometimes listing fees.

Why are they such a hit? For consumers, they offer a wide product range and competitive prices. For sellers, they provide access to a large customer base without needing to build one's own e-commerce infrastructure.

But, is this the step forward for you? Do you even need it? Let's break down, once and for all, the debate between online marketplaces and offline selling.

Online Marketplaces vs Offline Selling

- **Reach**: Online stores can serve customers nationwide or even globally. Offline stores are limited to local foot traffic.

- **Operating hours**: Online stores can operate 24x7. Offline stores have limited hours.

- **Overhead**: Online operations often have lower overhead costs, eliminating expenses like rent for prime locations.

- **Inventory**: Online stores can offer a wider range of products without physical space constraints. Offline selling is limited by shelf-space.

- **Data and analytics**: Online operations provide detailed insights into customer behaviour through analytics. In offline tracking, it is more challenging to narrow down the metrics and less precise.

- **Customer interaction**: Offline selling allows face-to-face interactions, building personal relationships. Online stores rely on digital communication and reviews for trust-building.

Having said that, I am not here to paint all roses and unicorns. Here's the unfiltered package you sign up for with online marketplaces—it offers several advantages, but also comes with a few drawbacks.

Pros and Cons of Selling on Online Marketplaces

Pros:

- Instant access to a large customer base.

- Lower entry barriers compared to setting up an independent e-commerce site.

- The built-in trust factor of established platforms.

- Simplified logistics and payment processing.

- Opportunity to test new products with minimal risk.

Cons:

- High competition, leading to potential price wars.

- Platform fees and commissions can eat into profits.

However, the purpose of this chapter is to help you navigate through the cons and maximize your business. You can cover the platform fees and commissions by setting up your pricing calculatedly. Similarly, marketing can help you stand out in high competition and drive more sales. This is what I'll discuss in some time.

12.2 Top Online Marketplaces in India

India's e-commerce market extends far beyond Amazon and Flipkart. You'll find a range of online marketplaces, each catering to specific niches, audiences, and business models. Let's look at some of the key categories and top marketplaces.

General E-commerce

- **Amazon India**: Offers a vast range of products across categories.

- **Flipkart**: Home-grown platform known for electronics and fashion.
- **Meesho**: Social commerce platform enabling small businesses and individuals to sell online.
- **JioMart**: Reliance's e-commerce venture focusing on groceries and daily essentials.
- **Snapdeal**: Focuses on value-for-money products across various categories.
- **Paytm Mall**: E-commerce arm of the popular digital payments platform.

Fashion and Lifestyle

- **Myntra**: Specializes in fashion, accessories, and lifestyle products.
- **Nykaa Fashion**: Fashion arm of the beauty retailer, offering curated clothing and accessories.
- **Tata CLiQ Luxury**: Luxury fashion and lifestyle products from premium brands.
- **Ajio**: Reliance Retail's fashion and lifestyle e-commerce platform.
- **LimeRoad**: Community driven fashion platform with a focus on women's wear.

Grocery and Food

- **Blinkit (formerly Grofers)**: Focuses on quick delivery of groceries and essentials.
- **Zepto**: Pioneer in ten-minute delivery of groceries and daily essentials.
- **BigBasket**: Comprehensive online grocery store with a wide product range.
- **JioMart**: Reliance's grocery platform integrating local kirana stores.

- **Zomato**: Restaurant discovery and food delivery platform.
- **Swiggy**: Restaurant food delivery and grocery service.
- **Dunzo**: Hyperlocal delivery service for food, groceries, and more.

Travel and Hospitality

- **MakeMyTrip**: Comprehensive travel booking platform for flights, hotels, and packages.
- **Yatra**: Travel services including flights, hotels, and holiday packages.
- **Cleartrip**: User-friendly interface for booking flights, hotels, and activities.
- **OYO Rooms**: Budget hotel chain and booking platform.
- **Treebo Hotels**: Branded budget hotels across India.
- **Airbnb India**: Peer-to-peer lodging and experience booking platform.

Online Pharmacies

- **PharmEasy**: E-pharmacy with doorstep delivery of medicines and diagnostics services.
- **TATA 1mg**: Online pharmacy and healthcare information platform.
- **Netmeds**: Online pharmacy offering medicines and health products.

Home Decor and Furnishings

- **Pepperfry**: Furniture and home decor marketplace.
- **Urban Ladder**: Curated selection of furniture and home decor items.
- **HomeLane**: End-to-end interior design and execution platform.

B2B Marketplaces

- **IndiaMART**: B2B platform connecting buyers with suppliers across industries.
- **Udaan**: B2B trade platform for small and medium businesses.
- **Moglix**: B2B e-commerce platform for industrial tools and equipment.
- **TradeIndia**: B2B marketplace for manufacturers, suppliers, and exporters.
- **Power2SME**: Procurement platform for raw materials and products for SMEs.
- **Wholesalebox**: B2B platform focusing on fashion and lifestyle products.

Electronics and Gadgets

- **Croma**: Tata Group's electronics retail chain with an online presence.
- **Reliance Digital**: Electronics and home appliances from Reliance Retail.
- **Vijay Sales**: Multi-brand electronics retailer with online and offline presence.

Beauty and Personal Care

- **Nykaa**: Multi-brand beauty and personal care retailer.
- **Purplle**: Online beauty and personal care products marketplace.
- **HealthKart**: Health and nutrition-focused e-commerce platform.
- **BeautyBebo**: Online retailer for beauty and skincare products.
- **MyGlamm**: Beauty products brand with its own e-commerce platform.

Note: This list is not comprehensive. There are many other niche online marketplaces.

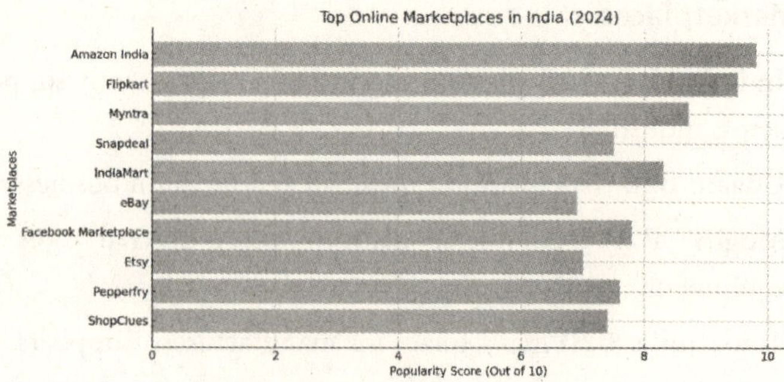

Image source: Shiprocket.in[4]

12.3 The Rise of Quick Commerce

When talking about grocery and food, I can't miss talking about quick commerce (or q-commerce), which is the next evolution in online marketplaces. It promises delivery within 10–30 minutes, fundamentally changing how Indians shop for everyday essentials. This model has gained massive traction, especially in urban areas where speed and convenience drive purchasing decisions.

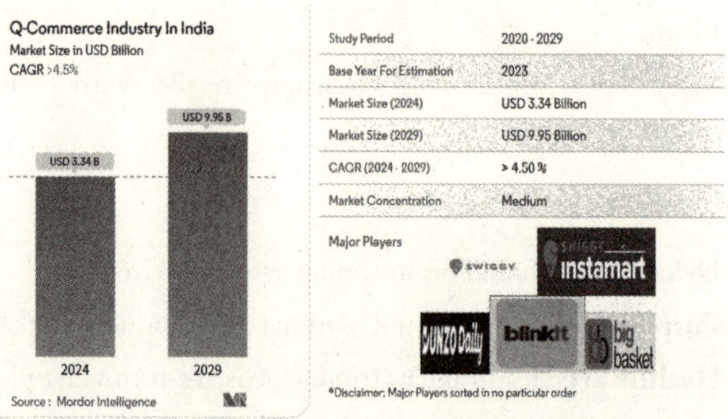

Image source: Mordor Intelligence[5]

Key players like Blinkit, Zepto, and Swiggy Instamart operate through dark stores—small warehouses strategically located across cities. These stores stock 1,000–2,000 high-demand items, allowing for ultra-fast delivery.

For sellers, quick commerce offers unique opportunities:

- Higher margins due to premium pricing for convenience.
- Faster inventory turnover.
- Reduced storage costs.
- Access to impulse buyers.
- Real-time demand insights.

However, it also comes with challenges:

- Strict inventory management requirements.
- Need for consistent stock availability.
- Higher quality standards due to quick turnover.
- Complex logistics coordination.

If you sell everyday essentials, FMCG products, or perishables, quick commerce platforms could be a great addition to your marketplace strategy. The key is maintaining tight inventory control and ensuring your products meet the platform's quick-turnaround requirements.

12.4 Which marketplace is right for you?

Selling on the most popular marketplace might seem like a no-brainer. After all, more traffic means more potential customers, right? Not necessarily.

A great example of a brand that faced challenges after trying to expand into multiple platforms is Burberry. The brand once well-known for its close ties to British luxury fashion started to suffer in the early 2000s, when its products became too easily obtained, which encouraged imitation and damaged the brand's reputation.

Burberry lost its exclusivity and saw a decline in sales as a result of its attempt to be available on many platforms and appeal to a wide audience.

In order to recover, the brand then made the decision to concentrate its approach by combining its online and offline presence, highlighting exclusivity, and utilizing specific digital channels. This helped reestablish their sales growth and restore their premium image.

Image source: Screengrab from Bloomberg Television video item entitled 'Burberry Cuts Full-Year Profit Forecast as Sales Decline'[6]

The platform with the most visitors might not align with your products or target audience. Your ideal customers may shop elsewhere.

The visibility and potential growth of a brand gets restricted when it is only available on one platform. According to recent insights, sellers that use multiple platforms can boost sales by up to 190 per cent since they can take advantage of various market dynamics and reach a larger audience. Furthermore, 42 per cent of online shoppers routinely purchase on at least two marketplaces, therefore making it critical to diversify your presence to increase customer acquisition.[7]

It's worth noting that you're not limited to just one platform. If you go this route, tools like Sellbrite or ChannelAdvisor can make managing multiple platforms simpler.

In the end, your choice should match your business model, products, and growth plans. Let me explain how you can find the right marketplace for your business.

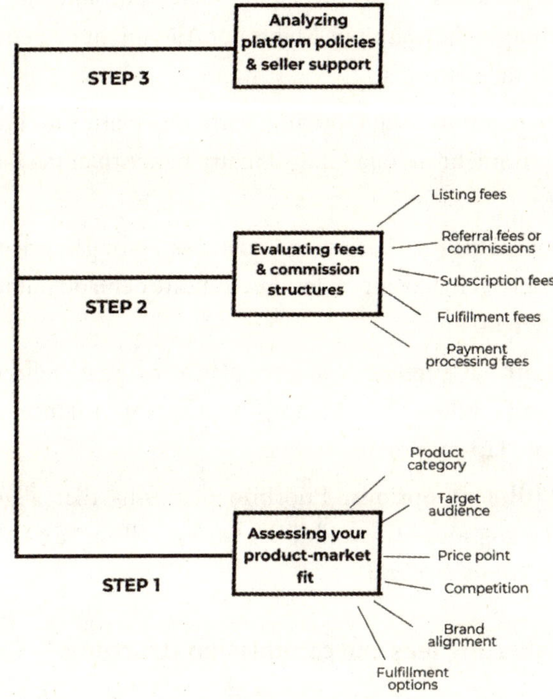

Image source: Author's illustration

12.4.1 Assessing Your Product-Market Fit

Your products need to align with the marketplace and its audience.

- **Product category:** Specialized products work better on niche platforms. For example, handmade crafts fit Etsy India better than Amazon.

- **Target audience:** Understand where your audience shops. Selling trendy fashion? Myntra or Ajio might be better than general platforms.

- **Price point:** Align pricing with the platform. Premium items might fit Tata CLiQ Luxury better than mass-market sites.

- **Competition:** Analyse competitors' ratings, prices, and reviews. High competition can indicate demand but requires differentiation.

- **Brand alignment:** Choose platforms that reflect your brand's values. Eco-friendly brands, for instance, should avoid fast-fashion platforms.

- **Fulfilment options:** Prioritize platforms that align with your logistics. Amazon's FBA works well for fast shipping, but comes at a cost.

12.4.2 Evaluating fees and commission structures

Marketplace fees vary widely and affect your bottom line. For example, Amazon charges 3–38 per cent referral fees, while Flipkart charges 2–25 per cent.

Common fees include:

- **Listing fees:** Charged for adding items.
- **Referral/commission fees:** A percentage of each sale.

- **Subscription fees:** Monthly/annual seller account charges.
- **Fulfilment fees:** For using platform logistics.
- **Payment processing fees:** Charges for transactions.

List all fees, calculate totals for your average order value, and compare across platforms. Sometimes, platforms with higher fees and a larger, more relevant audience can yield better overall returns.

Analysing platform policies and seller support

Marketplace policies and support quality are critical to your success.

- **Policies**: Most platforms have rules for shipping, quality, and returns. For example, Amazon expects 95 per cent on-time delivery, while Flipkart's return policies might lead to higher returns for you.
- **Seller protection**: Some platforms favour buyers (e.g., Amazon's A-to-Z Guarantee), but others, like Meesho, offer return shipping insurance.
- **Seller support**: Reach out to platforms to gauge response times. Some offer account managers for high sellers, while others rely on forums or email.

Pro tip: Look for platforms with active seller communities. These can be goldmines of information and support, especially when you're just starting out.

12.5 Marketing on Marketplaces: The Visibility Pyramid

The Visibility Pyramid is a framework we've used for years to help SMBs succeed on online marketplaces. It's a step-by-step approach to increasing your visibility and sales. Each level builds on the one below it, creating a solid foundation for your marketing efforts.

There are six levels, including zero. Let's go through each level one by one.

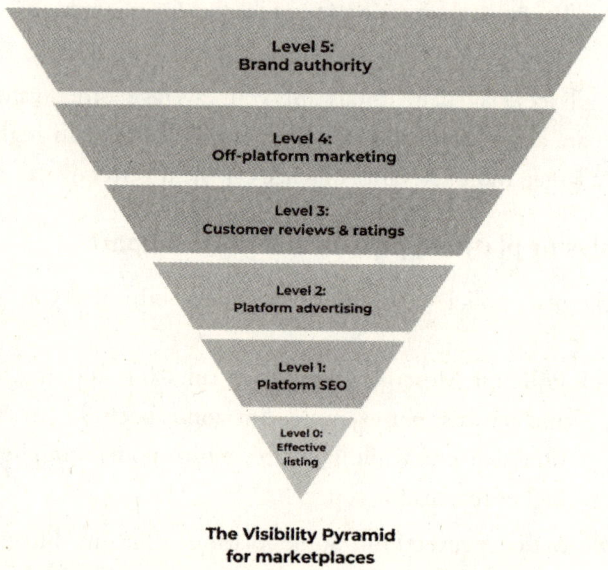

Image source: Author's illustration

Level 0: Effective Listing

A well-crafted listing helps shoppers find your product and convinces them to buy. I've covered the basics of creating a product listing in the previous section.

In general, a good listing starts with accurate product categorization, which ensures you're in the right digital 'aisle'. Clear, informative titles and descriptions help both search algorithms and customers understand what you're selling. High-quality images showcase your product effectively, while competitive pricing and clear shipping information set the right expectations. Proper inventory management prevents disappointed customers due to out-of-stock items.

Even the best marketing strategies can't compensate for a poor listing. It's like trying to sell a great product in a messy, disorganized store—you're fighting an uphill battle from the start. This is why getting the product listing right is level zero.

Products that match the tag 'Men's active wear white' showcasing how effective listing can help you rank. Image source: Myntra.com

Level 1: Platform SEO

Platform SEO ensures your product listings are optimized. It focuses on understanding and leveraging the unique algorithms of each marketplace to improve your product's visibility in search results.

Unlike traditional SEO, platform SEO considers factors specific to e-commerce, such as sales history, review ratings, and inventory levels.

Acing platform SEO can dramatically increase your organic traffic and sales without additional ad spend. Here's what you need to focus on:

- **Keyword research and placement**: Use marketplace-specific tools to identify high-converting search terms. Place primary keywords in titles, secondary in bullet points, and long-tail in descriptions. For example, Amazon's Search Term Report can reveal valuable keywords your customers are using.

- **Category and subcategory optimization**: Each subcategory has its own bestseller list. Sometimes, ranking high in a less competitive subcategory can drive more sales than ranking low in a popular one. Analyse your product's performance in different categories to find the sweet spot.

- **Review velocity**: The rate at which you accumulate reviews impacts search ranking. Implement a systematic review request process in your post-purchase communication. Be careful to follow marketplace guidelines (incentivizing reviews is often against the rules).

- **Sales velocity**: Recent sales history influences ranking. Use promotional campaigns strategically to boost short-term sales and improve ranking. This creates a positive feedback loop—better ranking leads to more sales, which further improves ranking.

- **Click-through rate (CTR) optimization**: A higher CTR signals relevance to marketplace algorithms. Test different main images, titles, and pricing to improve your CTR. Even small improvements can impact your visibility big time.

- **Conversion rate optimization**: High conversion rates improve search ranking. A/B test your bullet points and product descriptions to identify what converts best. Pay attention to your pricing strategy; the lowest price doesn't always win.

- **Mobile optimization**: With the majority of the Indian e-commerce traffic coming from mobile, ensure your listings are mobile-friendly. Use short paragraphs, clear headings, and mobile-optimized images.

- **Competitive indexing**: Identify top-ranking competitor Amazon Standard Identification Numbers (ASINs) and ensure your listings are indexed for the same key terms.

This helps you appear in the 'Compare with similar items' section.

- **Seasonal keyword optimization**: Update your keywords to align with seasonal trends and shopping events, such as Diwali or summer sales. Plan these updates in advance to capture early seasonal traffic.

- **Backend search terms**: Use the backend search terms field effectively. Include synonyms, common misspellings, and related terms that didn't fit in your visible content. On Amazon, you typically get 250 characters; use them wisely.

Implementing these steps requires consistent effort and analysis. Regularly audit your listings against these points and adjust based on performance data.

Each marketplace has its unique algorithm, so what works on Amazon might not work on Flipkart. Stay informed about platform-specific best practices, and be ready to adapt your strategy accordingly.

Level 2: Platform Advertising

Platform advertising allows you to promote your products directly within the marketplace. It complements your organic efforts by increasing visibility, especially for new products or in competitive categories. This helps particularly when you've optimized your listings and SEO but need an extra push to reach more potential customers.

Marketplace advertising typically operates on a pay-per-click (PPC) model, where you bid on keywords or product placements. You're charged only when a shopper clicks on your ad, making it a measurable and often cost-effective way to drive traffic to your listings.

Here are some common types of ads include:

- **Sponsored products**: These ads display individual product listings within search results and on product detail pages. They're marked as 'Sponsored' or 'Ad'. You bid on keywords relevant to your product, and your ad appears when shoppers use those or related terms in their search.

- **Sponsored brands**: These more prominent ads feature your brand logo, a custom headline, and multiple product images. They typically appear at the top of search results or in banner positions. These ads help build brand awareness and can drive traffic to your brand store or a custom landing page.

- **Product display ads**: These appear on related product detail pages, often under sections like 'Customers also viewed' or 'Related to items you've viewed'. They're particularly effective for cross-selling or targeting competitors' product pages.

- **Video ads**: Some platforms like Amazon offer video ad options. These can appear in search results or on product detail pages, allowing you to showcase your product in action.

- **Sponsored display ads**: These retargeting ads can reach shoppers who've viewed your products or similar items, both on and off the marketplace platform.

Each ad type serves different purposes in your marketing funnel, from brand awareness to direct sales conversion. Your choice depends on your specific goals, budget, and the stage of your product's lifecycle.

Image source: Google search results

The first row of these marketplaces is filled with sponsored ads that you can benefit from the purpose of ranking.

Level 3: Customer Reviews and Ratings

Customer reviews and ratings are your social proof. They build trust, improve visibility, and directly impact your sales. Products with more positive reviews consistently outperform those without, even at higher price points. Here's how to make the most of them:

- **Solicit reviews ethically**: Most marketplaces have a 'Request a Review' button. Use it consistently. You can also follow up via email, but be careful not to incentivize reviews. That's against most marketplace policies.

- **Timing matters**: Wait until the customer has had time to use the product before requesting a review. For a t-shirt, a week might be enough. For a gadget, wait two weeks.

- **Respond to all reviews**: Yes, even the negative ones. Be professional, empathetic, and solution-oriented. A well-handled negative review can actually boost customer confidence.

- **Use reviews for product development**: Pay attention to common praises or complaints. They're free market research. I've seen businesses completely turn around by addressing frequent criticisms in their product reviews.

- **Leverage positive reviews**: If you get a particularly glowing review, consider reaching out to the customer for permission to use it in your marketing materials.

- **Handle negative reviews proactively**: If you notice a trend in negative reviews, address the issue immediately. Update your product, adjust your description, or improve your packaging. Then, mention these improvements in your listing.

- **Understand the impact on SEO**: Reviews often contain keywords that help your product appear in more search results. They also improve your conversion rate, indirectly boosting your search ranking.

The goal isn't just to get more reviews, but to consistently deliver a product and experience worth raving about. Focus on that, and the positive reviews will follow naturally.

The Story of Popflex

Cassey Ho, the founder of Popflex, has transformed the fitness apparel industry by inviting her community into her design process. Through engaging videos on platforms like YouTube and Instagram, she takes her audience behind the scenes, sharing the journey of creating new styles based on their feedback. The brand has seen remarkable growth, with a reported 300 per cent increase in sales from 2020 to 2021, largely attributed to its responsiveness to customer concerns.

In her videos, Cassey showcases initial sketches and prototypes, encouraging her followers to share their thoughts on fit, colour, and overall design. For instance, when customers expressed the need for more inclusive sizing, Cassey didn't just hear their concerns—she documented her entire journey of revising patterns and testing new fabrics to create a better fit.

By valuing customer input and highlighting how their suggestions shape the final products, Cassey has cultivated a loyal community that feels invested in the Popflex brand. This approach has turned feedback into a powerful tool for growth, showcasing how listening to customers can lead to successful and beloved products.

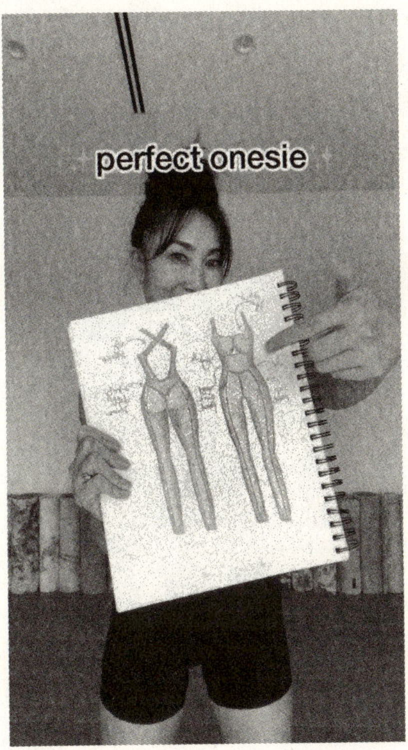

Image source: Blogilates on Instagram, via Pinterest[8]

Level 4: Off-Platform Marketing

Off-platform marketing extends your reach beyond the marketplace. It aids in creating multiple touchpoints with potential customers and driving targeted traffic to your product listings. This helps when you've maxed out your on-platform efforts and need to tap into new customer pools.

Here's how you can leverage off-platform marketing:

- **Social media marketing**: Platforms like Instagram and Facebook are goldmines for product discovery. Create engaging content that showcases your products in use. Use high-quality images and short videos to capture attention. Don't just push sales; provide value. If you're selling kitchen gadgets, share quick recipes or cooking tips.

Image source: Nikki.K clothing Instagram page, 2024[9]

Brands using social media to gather more eyeballs send traffic to their respective marketplaces.

- **Google ads**: Use Google Shopping ads to appear in product searches outside the marketplace. This can be particularly effective for branded searches or specific product types.

- **Influencer partnerships**: Collaborate with influencers whose audience aligns with your target market. I've seen small businesses explode overnight with the right influencer partnership. Start with micro-influencers (10,000–100,000 followers) in your niche. They often have higher engagement rates and more affordable rates.

- **Content marketing**: Blog posts, YouTube videos, or podcasts can position you as an authority in your field. If you sell fitness equipment, create workout guides or nutrition tips. Link back to your marketplace listings where relevant.

- **Email marketing**: Build an email list through your social media following or website. Use email to nurture relationships, share exclusive deals, and drive traffic to your listings during sales events.

- **Retargeting**: Use pixel tracking to retarget visitors from your website or social media to your marketplace listings. This keeps your products top-of-mind and can significantly boost conversion rates.

The key to off-platform marketing is consistency and integration. Ensure your branding and messaging are consistent across all channels. And always track your efforts. Use unique links or promo codes to measure which off-platform strategies are driving the most sales.

Level 5: Brand Authority

Brand authority is the pinnacle of the Visibility Pyramid—it's when customers seek out your products specifically, regardless of marketplace rankings or ads. At this level, you're beyond selling products; you're selling a story, a lifestyle, an experience.

While building brand authority is a subject of its own, here are some fundamental tips you can follow:

- **Consistent brand voice**: Develop a unique tone and style that resonates with your target audience. Use this consistently across all your communications—from product descriptions to customer service interactions.

- **Brand storytelling**: Share the story behind your brand. Why did you start? What problems are you solving? People connect with stories, not just products.

- **Quality customer service**: Go above and beyond in your customer interactions. Prompt, helpful responses build trust and loyalty. I've seen brands turn one-time buyers into lifelong advocates through exceptional service.

- **Thought leadership**: Share your expertise through blog posts, interviews, or speaking engagements. If you sell eco-friendly products, become a vocal advocate for sustainability in your industry.

- **Community building**: Create a space for your customers to connect with each other. This could be a Facebook group, a subreddit, or an annual event. Foster discussions, share exclusive content, and make your customers feel part of something bigger.

- **Innovation and product development**: Continuously improve your products based on customer feedback. Launch new products that solve emerging problems in your niche. This keeps your brand fresh and relevant.

- **Collaborations and limited editions**: Partner with other brands or artists for limited edition products. This creates buzz and gives customers a reason to keep checking back with your brand.

- **Social responsibility**: Align your brand with causes that matter to your audience. Whether it's environmental sustainability, social justice, or local community support, show that your brand stands for more than just profit.

Building brand authority takes time and consistent effort. But once established, it provides a competitive edge that's hard to replicate. Your products become more than just items. They become part of your customers' identities.

12.6 Checklist for Local Businesses to Sell on Online Marketplaces

- ✓ Research and choose suitable marketplaces for your products.
- ✓ Gather necessary documents (GST, PAN, bank details) for seller registration.
- ✓ Create and optimize your seller account on chosen marketplaces.
- ✓ Conduct keyword research for your product categories.
- ✓ Optimize product titles with relevant keywords.
- ✓ Create detailed and benefit-focused product descriptions.
- ✓ Take high-quality product photos from multiple angles.
- ✓ Set competitive pricing based on market research and profit margins.
- ✓ Implement inventory management system across all platforms.
- ✓ Set up fulfilment strategy (self-shipping or platform fulfilment).
- ✓ Regularly update listings based on performance data.
- ✓ Start small with sponsored ads on marketplaces.
- ✓ Develop a social media strategy to drive off-platform traffic.

- ✓ Create content (blog posts, videos) to establish industry authority.
- ✓ Engage with customer reviews, both positive and negative.
- ✓ Monitor and adjust advertising campaigns based on performance.
- ✓ Continuously analyse competitor strategies and adapt accordingly.
- ✓ Regularly audit your seller account health and address any issues promptly.
- ✓ Stay updated with marketplace policy changes and new features.

13

Revamp Your Reach: Leveraging OTTs, Webinars, and More

'THE DIFFERENCE BETWEEN ORDINARY AND extraordinary is that little extra,' said Jimmy Johnson (American football coach).[1]

As a start-up or business founder, you pour your heart and soul into your digital marketing plan. You tick all the right boxes—optimize for SEO, maintain a consistent social media presence, run paid ads, and analyse metrics. Yet, the growth seems negligible, and it's not what you expected. You might wonder:

- Why does engagement plateau despite regular posting?
- Why do paid ads yield only lukewarm returns?
- Why do others in your niche seem to soar while you're stuck in the basics?

In reality, getting your fundamentals right helps you rise above the noise, but staying there makes you just another voice. To grow beyond average and become a brand, you need to aim higher. You need a strategy that dares to be different, a plan that resonates deeply with your audience and sets you apart.

I have spent the previous chapters detailing SEO, PPC, influencer marketing, and other foundational digital marketing channels. These channels form the core digital strategy for most businesses—and rightfully so.

Small businesses with tight budgets often focus on select channels to maximize their immediate ROI. However, as your business grows, sticking to just a handful of channels can limit your potential.

Why? Because each marketing channel only taps into certain segments of your audience and has a saturation point. Expanding your digital presence across multiple channels ensures you reach untapped audiences, diversify your risk, and create multiple touchpoints to drive consistent engagement. For example, while Instagram might help you engage a younger demographic, webinars or email marketing could be the gateway to capturing professionals or B2B clients.

Let's take the example of Swiggy. They don't just excel at Instagram marketing; they dominate Google search results, run engaging YouTube campaigns, and create viral content on X. Or, take CRED. Beyond their memorable TV ads, they've aced push notifications, email marketing, and influencer partnerships. Nykaa started with just Instagram and Facebook, but today, they dominate everywhere—from SEO to WhatsApp marketing to marketplace optimization.

This multichannel presence isn't accidental. These brands recognized that limiting yourself to just the essentials eventually leads to a growth ceiling. To grow spectacularly, your marketing must extend beyond the basics.

Now, there are countless ways to think about marketing. You could categorize it by psychology, user behaviour, or even technologies like programmatic advertising. However, for start-ups ready to scale, I recommend focusing on practical, actionable channels that drive measurable results.

That's why I believe six advanced marketing channels stand out for businesses looking to move beyond the basics:

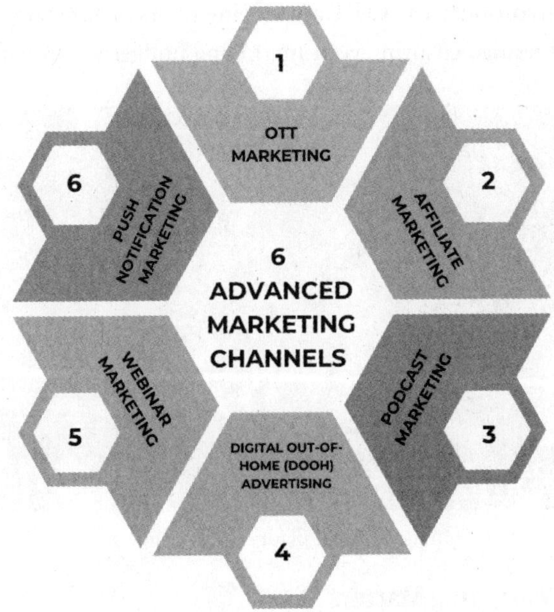

Image source: Author's illustration

These channels matter because they align with emerging consumer behaviours and provide opportunities to stand out while others compete on saturated platforms. Each opens fresh territories for capturing and converting your audience.

In this chapter, I'll show you how to evaluate and implement these advanced marketing channels. You'll learn when to adopt them, how to measure their impact, and real examples of brands succeeding with each approach.

13.1 OTT Marketing

Over-the-top (OTT) marketing lets you place your brand directly on platforms like Netflix, JioHotstar, Hoichoi, and Amazon Prime Video, where your audience is actively engaged. With the shift from traditional TV to streaming, this is an opportunity you can't ignore.

Unlike traditional TV, OTT advertising offers precise targeting and measurable results, ensuring your marketing budget works harder.

Image source: Gadgets360.com[2]

Why OTT Marketing Matters

Audiences have moved from cable to streaming; these platforms dominate screens in households across demographics.

Picture this: during a high-stakes IPL match, millions are glued to their screens, cheering for their favourite team. Over-the-Top marketing lets your brand join the action, reaching viewers during these high-impact moments. It's more than just the visibility; it's really about being relevant when your audience is most engaged.

How OTT Advertising Works

Ads are delivered via internet-connected devices like smart TVs, mobile phones, and laptops.

These ads can be pre-roll clips that appear before the content, mid-roll ads during breaks, or even static banners within the app. The targeting capabilities are game-changing—you can narrow your audience by location, age, interests, or even what they're watching.

Imagine you run a premium tea brand targeting millennials. You could place a pre-roll ad during a trending show like Gullak on SonyLIV, instantly connecting with audiences who appreciate nostalgic, homegrown stories—just like your product.

When Should You Use OTT Marketing?

This is ideal when you're ready to scale beyond basic channels. It's particularly effective for businesses in e-commerce, fintech, edtech, or lifestyle industries. If your target audience spends hours streaming and your brand story thrives on visuals, OTT is your next growth lever.

Consider a personal finance app that targets working professionals. By advertising during popular OTT content that focuses on productivity or money management, the app can reach users already primed to consider financial planning. The result? Increased sign-ups from high-value customers.

How to Get Started with OTT Marketing

- **Know your audience**: Where do they stream? What content do they love? Think regional languages, niche genres, and even live events.

- **Pick the right platform**: Want younger audiences? Go for platforms like YouTube or JioHotstar. Family-focused? Try SonyLIV or Zee5.

- **Create impactful ads**: Think crisp, relatable, and visually striking. Imagine you're speaking directly to the viewer—because you are.

- **Experiment and optimize**: Start with a small budget, analyse the results, and refine your approach.

13.2 Affiliate Marketing

Affiliate marketing allows you to leverage partnerships to drive sales and leads for your business. By collaborating with affiliates who promote your product or service, you only pay for results. This makes it one of the most cost-effective channels for scaling your business.

Why Affiliate Marketing Matters

It's simple—affiliate marketing broadens your reach without upfront ad spend. The global affiliate marketing industry is worth USD 27.8 billion, with a 17.8 per cent year-on-year growth. The industry is expected to flourish, turning its 2024 valuation of USD 32.3 billion into USD 48 billion by 2027.

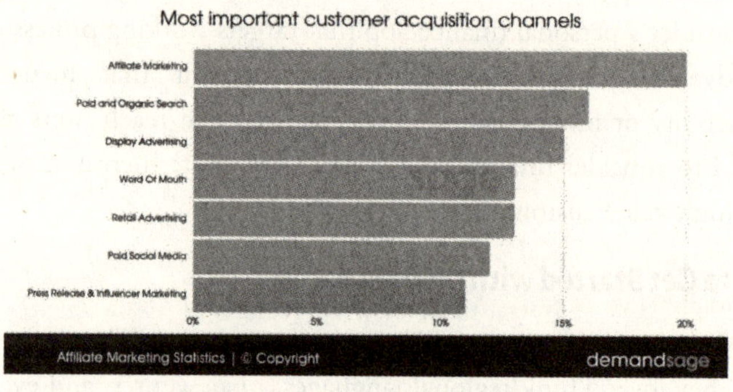

Image source: Demandsage.com[3]

Affiliates use their platforms—blogs, YouTube channels, or social media—to share your brand with their audiences. Every time they drive a purchase or lead, you pay them a commission. This performance-based model means you're only investing in proven results.

How Affiliate Marketing Works

You set up an affiliate programme that offers a commission for every sale or lead generated. Affiliates then promote your products using their unique tracking links. When someone clicks the link and completes the desired action, the affiliate earns their reward.

For example, let's say you run an edtech platform. By partnering with education-focused YouTubers, you can have them share reviews or tutorials of your product, targeting students and professionals looking to upskill.

When to Use Affiliate Marketing

Affiliate marketing is ideal for start-ups looking to scale with limited resources. I have seen it work exceptionally well for e-commerce, SaaS, and subscription-based businesses. If you have a clear value proposition and a competitive commission structure, affiliates will eagerly promote your brand.

Take a fitness equipment company as an example. They could drive significant traffic and sales without spending heavily on ads, simply by partnering with fitness influencers. Affiliates benefit from commissions, while the company gains access to highly engaged audiences.

How to Get Started with Affiliate Marketing

- **Set goals**: Define whether you want to drive sales, generate leads, or increase brand awareness.

- **Pick a platform**: Use networks like Commission Junction, ShareASale, or vCommission to connect with affiliates and manage performance.

- **Attract affiliates**: Promote your programme through your website and outreach, offering competitive commissions and clear guidelines.

- **Provide resources**: Share banners, email templates, and product descriptions to help affiliates promote effectively.

- **Track and optimize**: Monitor performance using tracking links and analytics to refine strategies and improve results.

13.3 Podcast Marketing

Podcast marketing helps you connect with audiences who value authentic, in-depth conversations. With millions tuning in during commutes, workouts, and downtime, podcasts offer a unique opportunity to engage listeners when they are most attentive and receptive to your message.

Why Podcasts Are an Opportunity You Can't Ignore

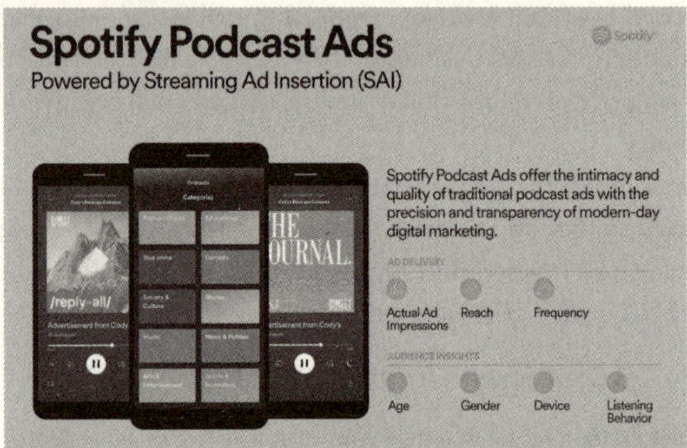

Image source: TheMediaAnt.com[4]

Podcasts allow your brand to build trust over extended listening sessions. Unlike the fleeting nature of ads on other platforms, podcasts create space for your message to resonate deeply with the audience. When you sponsor a podcast or host your own, you're not just running ads—you're building a relationship.

Take Indian shows like *The Ranveer Show* or *Paisa Vaisa*. These podcasts cater to niche audiences who are already invested in self-growth or financial advice. This makes them an ideal platform for brands targeting those segments, ensuring your message reaches people who care about it.

How Podcast Marketing Works

There are two main approaches: sponsoring existing podcasts or creating your own.

- **Sponsoring podcasts**: This involves partnering with podcast hosts to feature your brand in their episodes. These mentions can come as pre-roll ads, mid-roll segments, or even conversational integrations. For example, a productivity app could sponsor a business-focused podcast, ensuring their product gets discussed naturally in the context of the show.

- **Creating your own podcast**: This is ideal for businesses that want to establish thought leadership. Imagine launching a podcast about the challenges of scaling a start-up, where you interview successful founders or share actionable insights. Over time, your podcast can become a trusted resource for your audience while driving awareness for your brand.

When Should You Use Podcast Marketing?

Podcast marketing works best for brands targeting niche audiences who value expertise and storytelling—B2B companies, edtech platforms, and premium consumer brands often benefit the most. If your product solves specific pain points or appeals to a passionate community, podcasts are an excellent fit.

Consider a wellness tech company looking to reach fitness enthusiasts. Sponsoring a podcast focused on mindfulness or healthy living ensures the brand connects with listeners already interested in their offerings, driving meaningful engagement.

How to Get Started with Podcast Marketing

- **Identify the right podcasts**: Look for shows with an audience that aligns with your target demographic. Consider the show's tone, listener engagement, and reputation.

- **Craft authentic messaging**: Podcast audiences value sincerity. Ensure your ad or message feels organic and relatable within the context of the episode.

- **Track performance**: Use unique discount codes, tracking links, or listener surveys to measure the effectiveness of your campaigns. This helps you refine your strategy over time.

13.4 Digital Out-of-Home (DOOH) Advertising

Digital Out-of-Home advertising transforms traditional billboards into dynamic, interactive digital screens placed in high-traffic public spaces. From bustling metro stations to busy shopping malls, it ensures your brand reaches the right audience at the right time, blending visual appeal with advanced targeting capabilities.

Image source: MeraHoardings.com

Why DOOH Matters

Imagine your brand showcased on a vibrant digital screen at a crowded airport or during rush hour at a metro station—DOOH brings your business into the public eye, creating a powerful physical presence. Unlike static billboards, it allows real-time updates and tailored messaging, making your campaigns as agile as your business needs.

For instance, DLF malls in Delhi, which see millions of visitors daily, provide an excellent backdrop for impactful DOOH campaigns. During the festive season, an e-commerce start-up could showcase

Diwali discounts on digital screens at DLF malls, attracting shoppers to their online store.

How DOOH Advertising Works

Direct Out-of-Home campaigns rely on programmatic technology and advanced digital infrastructure to deliver targeted, impactful advertisements. Here's how it works in practice.

- **Buying ad slots**: Programmatic platforms like Lemma or VIOOH allow you to select and purchase digital screen placements across locations based on your campaign needs.
- **Scheduling with precision**: You can time your ads to run during peak activity periods, such as morning and evening rush hours, maximizing visibility.
- **Geo-targeting and demographics**: Using location data, you can ensure your ads are displayed where your target audience frequents, such as business districts or shopping centres.
- **Dynamic content updates**: The technology allows you to instantly change ad content based on real-time triggers like weather, events, or inventory levels.

For example, a food delivery service can use location-based targeting to display lunchtime offers near office clusters. Real-time analytics then track ad performance, helping you refine messaging and placement for better results.

When to Use DOOH Advertising

It is ideal for building brand awareness or promoting time-sensitive offers. It's especially impactful for start-ups in retail, entertainment, hospitality, and travel because of its ability to combine eye-catching visuals with real-time content delivery. Whether placed in malls, airports, or metro stations, DOOH ensures your message reaches audiences when they are most attentive.

Leveraging transit hubs and high-footfall zones enhances the flexibility of this channel. The ability to integrate dynamic and adaptive content, such as real-time updates or contextual triggers, makes DOOH stand out. This approach not only captures attention but also drives engagement by presenting relevant, timely, and location-aware messaging. With the right strategy, DOOH can seamlessly blend visibility and interaction into a cohesive brand experience.

How to Get Started with DOOH Advertising

- **Set goals**: Define objectives like brand awareness, store footfall, or promoting time-sensitive offers.

- **Select the right locations**: Target high-traffic areas like metro stations, malls, or airports, based on your audience and campaign goals.

- **Design engaging content**: Think up bold visuals with dynamic elements like real-time updates or event-specific messaging.

- **Use programmatic buying**: Automate ad placements and target specific demographics with platforms like Lemma or VIOOH.

- **Integrate channels**: Add QR codes, short URLs, or hashtags to connect offline ads to your digital platforms.

- **Track and optimize**: Monitor metrics like impressions and engagement using tools like Times OOH to refine your strategy.

13.5 Webinar Marketing

Webinar marketing is your chance to connect directly with your audience in real time while establishing yourself as an expert in your field. A well-executed webinar educates and engages attendees by addressing their specific challenges and guiding them toward solutions—*your* solutions. It's an opportunity to answer questions, address objections, and move your audience zone step closer to becoming loyal customers.

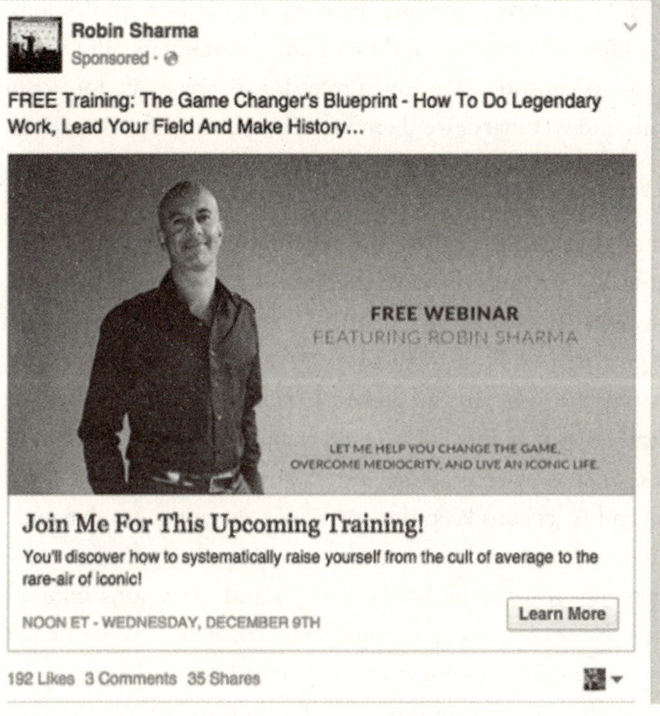

Source: Flowbox[5]

Why Webinar Marketing Works

Webinars give you a direct line to your audience, unlike traditional one-way marketing channels. They allow for interaction, whether it's through live Q and A sessions, polls, or practical demonstrations. These elements create a space where you're not just pitching a product— you're having a conversation.

When you engage personally with your audience, you build trust. You're no longer just a name or a brand; you're a person who understands their struggles and offers real solutions. Trust is invaluable, especially in a country like India, where relationships and recommendations often drive buying decisions.

With a massive, growing base of digital-first professionals in India—especially in tier-1 and tier-2 cities—webinars offer the perfect platform to capture attention. Professionals are eager for actionable insights, and webinars give them value in exchange for their time.

How Webinar Marketing Works

Webinar marketing begins with audience registration, where you promote the webinar through channels like email, social media, and your website. Interested participants sign up, giving you a pre-qualified list of potential leads.

During the webinar, you present content tailored to your audience's interests or pain points. This could include live product demos, case studies, or step-by-step guides. Interactive features like polls, surveys, and Q and A sessions keep the experience engaging and dynamic.

Unlike pre-recorded content, webinars allow for real-time engagement. You can address questions and objections immediately, making the session more personal and relatable. At the end of the webinar, you guide attendees to take the next step with a clear call-to-action, such as signing up for a free trial, downloading a resource, or booking a consultation.

When to Use Webinar Marketing

Webinars work best when your audience needs more than a simple advertisement; they need education, insight, and clarity. Use webinars when:

- **You're launching a complex product or service**: Webinars are great for explaining sophisticated offerings, such as SaaS tools or financial services, in a way that makes them easy to understand.
- **You want to establish yourself as an expert**: If you're in a competitive market, webinars allow you to stand out by showcasing your knowledge and unique approach.

- **You're targeting B2B or professional audiences**: In India, business owners, freelancers, and professionals value learning opportunities. A webinar on 'Tax Savings for Freelancers' or 'Scaling Your E-commerce Business' will resonate deeply with this crowd.

- **You need to build trust**: When your audience is sceptical or unfamiliar with your brand, a webinar offers the transparency and interaction needed to gain their confidence.

How to Get Started with Webinar Marketing

- **Set goals**: Decide whether your webinar aims to build brand awareness, generate leads, or drive sales.

- **Choose a topic**: Focus on solving a specific audience problem, like '5 Strategies to Cut Marketing Costs'.

- **Select a platform**: Use tools like Zoom or GoToWebinar with features like screen sharing and Q and A.

- **Promote effectively**: Use email, LinkedIn, and WhatsApp to highlight the webinar's value.

- **Prepare content**: Create a structured, actionable agenda with visuals and live interactions.

- **Test and practice**: Run a trial session to ensure the platform and tools work seamlessly.

- **Engage live**: Use polls, quizzes, and Q and A to encourage participation and maintain interest.

- **Follow up**: Send thank-you emails, recordings, and calls-to-action to nurture attendees.

13.6 Push Notification Marketing

Push notifications allow you to reach your audience instantly through their smartphones or web browsers. Whether it's a flash sale, an important update, or a personalized offer, push notifications deliver your message when your audience is most likely to engage.

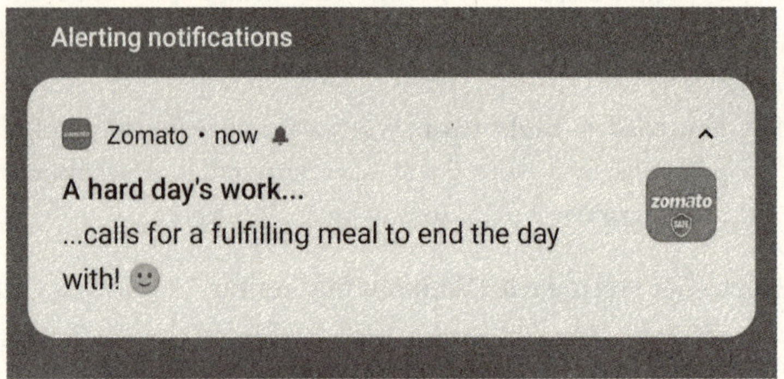

Image source: Barkha Kukreja, 2021[6]

Why Push Notification Marketing Matters

Push notifications create immediate visibility. Unlike emails or social media posts that might get lost in the shuffle, push notifications appear directly on your user's screen. They're hard to ignore and highly effective for driving quick actions.

In India, where mobile usage dominates, push notifications tap into the everyday habits of users. Whether reminding someone to complete their abandoned cart or notifying them of a nearby discount, they're a powerful tool for maintaining engagement in a competitive market.

How Push Notification Marketing Works

Push notifications are short, actionable alerts sent directly to users' devices via mobile apps or web browsers. These notifications are powered by push notification servers that interact with APIs and SDKs embedded within your app or site. Once a user opts in, their device is registered to receive updates.

Technically, notifications can be triggered by user actions—like abandoning a cart—or preset conditions such as location (via geofencing), app activity, or behavioural preferences. A notification server processes user data to deliver messages that align with their habits or location in real-time.

Platforms like Firebase or WebEngage enable brands to send and track these alerts, offering analytics on delivery rates, open rates, and user engagement. With this combination of real-time data and technical precision, push notifications create immediate, impactful touchpoints with your audience.

When to Use Push Notification Marketing

You can use push notifications when you want to:

- Promote time-sensitive offers like flash sales.

- Re-engage inactive users with personalized messages.

- Drive immediate actions, such as completing a booking or purchase.

Push notifications are particularly effective for e-commerce, food delivery, and subscription-based apps, where quick engagement is critical.

How to Get Started with Push Notification Marketing

- **Build a subscriber base**: Encourage users to opt-in for push notifications by highlighting the value they'll receive, such as exclusive offers or timely updates.

- **Segment your audience**: Use data like location, purchase history, or browsing behaviour to create targeted campaigns. Segmentation ensures that your messages are relevant and personalized.

- **Craft compelling messages**: Keep your notifications short, clear, and action-driven. Include a strong call to action and, if possible, add a sense of urgency.

- **Use automation tools**: Platforms like OneSignal or WebEngage allow you to automate and schedule push notifications, saving time while maximizing reach.

- **Analyse and optimize**: Track metrics like open rates, click-through rates, and conversions. Use these insights to refine your campaigns and improve their effectiveness.

Push notification marketing is a direct and impactful way to engage your audience. When done right, it can drive immediate actions, foster brand loyalty, and boost your overall marketing strategy.

13.7 How to Determine Which Digital Marketing Channel to Use?

Choosing the right digital marketing channel requires aligning your goals, audience, and resources. Instead of chasing trends, focus on where your audience is active and what will deliver the best ROI. Here's how.

13.7.1 Start with Clear Objectives

Define what you want to achieve beyond the basics. Are you aiming for deeper audience engagement? Push notifications and webinars can foster direct, real-time connections. Want to tell your story visually? Channels like OTT marketing are better suited. Each channel serves a unique purpose, so match your choice to your specific goals.

13.7.2 Understand Your Audience's Habits

Where does your audience spend their time? Over-the-top platforms like JioHotstar dominate entertainment, while professionals rely on podcasts during commutes for insights. Push notifications can target frequent app users who need reminders or real-time offers.

Dig into your audience data to determine which emerging behaviours align with the non-essential channels discussed in this chapter. Pick the platforms where your audience is active but not oversaturated.

13.7.3 Assess Your Budget and Resources

Evaluate the financial and operational costs of each channel—OTT and DOOH campaigns often demand higher budgets but offer significant visibility, while conversely, affiliate marketing and webinars can deliver measurable ROI at a lower cost.

For smaller budgets, starting with affiliate programmes or experimenting with push notifications can help you maintain control while testing new strategies.

13.7.4 Test Small, Then Scale

Run pilot campaigns on one or two advanced channels before committing larger resources. Start with limited ad spends or localized efforts. For example, test DOOH ads in high-traffic areas during peak seasons, or launch a single webinar targeting a specific audience segment. Use analytics tools to measure performance, refine your strategy, and scale only what's working.

13.7.5 Stay Adaptable

The 'what next' ladder isn't rigid; it's dynamic and evolves with your business growth and audience behaviour. As preferences shift, certain channels—like podcasts or push notifications—might gain prominence, while others lose relevance.

To climb effectively, you need to revisit your audience data regularly, analyse which platforms are yielding results, and uncover fresh opportunities through experimentation.

For example, adding channels like OTT ads or DOOH during peak seasons can open untapped audience segments.

The key is to evaluate performance continuously and stay agile, ensuring your marketing efforts remain impactful in a changing market.

13.8 Growth Needs More Than Just the Essentials

I don't want you to feel overwhelmed by a long checklist of tasks. The point here is simple: for your business to grow meaningfully, your marketing must grow too. Sticking to the basics will only take you so far. At some point, you'll need to step out of your comfort zone, explore new platforms, and find ways to stand out.

Think about the brands you admire—they didn't stick to one or two channels. They expanded intentionally, choosing platforms that fit their audience and goals at each stage. Growth doesn't have to mean doing everything at once. It could start small, like trying push notifications or hosting a webinar.

Growth is a journey, and every step—every new channel—brings you closer to your audience, strengthens your brand, and sets you up for long-term success. Now that you have the tools to stand out, it's time to put them into action.

14

Tailored Sectoral Strategies for Industry-Specific Success

'A SMART PLAYER KNOWS NOT EVERY BALL IS WORTH swinging at; success lies in choosing the right ones to play and the right ones to let pass.'[1] Despite us having dealt with various strategies and tactics of digital marketing, as a start-up founder or while building a brand, you need to take into account the intricacies as well as nuances of the sector in which your company operates. Each sector is unique in its own requirements. While it is not possible for us to deal with each and every sector, we have attempted to cover some of the prominent sectors and provided various tactics for them.

Educating and Influencing Its Way into a Successful Fitness Business

For example, imagine FitLife Equip, a fitness equipment start-up specializing in home workout gear like resistance bands, dumbbells, and compact exercise bikes. They've allocated a sizeable budget to digital marketing, promoting their products through Google Ads, Instagram, and Facebook. However, despite the heavy ad spend, their sales have been stagnant, and they're struggling to build momentum.

Problem: FitLife Equip is using general digital marketing tactics without tailoring them to the specific demands of the fitness sector, leading to inefficiencies and lost potential.

1. **Lack of customer testimonials and user-generated content**: In the fitness industry, credibility and customer trust are essential, as people want proof of product effectiveness. FitLife is running image ads without user testimonials, reviews, or success stories. By failing to showcase customer feedback or testimonials, they're unable to build trust.

2. **Neglecting influencer marketing**: Fitness is a highly visual, aspirational sector, where influencers and fitness coaches play a huge role in shaping consumer decisions. FitLife isn't engaging fitness influencers or trainers who could demonstrate the products in action, giving them credibility and encouraging their followers to try the equipment and a connect with fitness communities.

3. **Inadequate targeting for seasonal trends**: In fitness, customer demand often peaks in January (New Year resolutions), and in the summer (when people want to get in shape). FitLife has not addressed season-specific trends and, therefore, misses opportunities for higher sales. Its budget is evenly spread across the year, leading to reduced ad performance during peak demand times.

4. **Lack of product education content**: Fitness equipment can require guidance on correct usage, to prevent injury and ensure optimal results. FitLife doesn't provide educational content—such as video demonstrations, setup guides, or workout routines featuring their equipment—leaving potential customers uncertain about how to use the products. Without this support, customers may hesitate to purchase, opting instead for brands that help guide their fitness journey.

Outcome: Despite FitLife's heavy marketing investment, they see minimal returns because their approach doesn't consider fitness industry specifics. These gaps reduce customer confidence, limit brand reach, and lead to poor conversion rates, resulting in a waste of FitLife's marketing budget. This underscores the importance of using sector-specific tactics to connect effectively with the right audience and make the most of digital marketing efforts.

If we flip the script on all the problem points, these can be utilized as a customized marketing strategy for the fitness industry, enabling brands like FitLife to ace the digital marketing game through sectoral tactics.

We shall now see how the digital marketing tactics can be tailored to the specific needs and characteristics of different sectors. While some general strategies, like SEO and social media marketing, apply across industries, the execution varies based on the nature of the business, target audience, and sales cycle. Below are examples of how digital marketing tactics can be nuanced according to different sectors.

14.1 Real Estate: Focus on Lead Generation & Local SEO

Tactic: Lead Generation through Paid Ads and Landing Pages

- **Why:** Real estate businesses often rely heavily on lead generation to connect potential buyers or renters with agents or developers.

- **Execution:** Real estate companies may focus on creating high-converting landing pages with lead capture forms, offering incentives like 'Free Property Tour' or 'Exclusive Market Report' in exchange for contact information.

- **Example:** Running Facebook Ads or Google Ads targeting specific locations and demographics (e.g., high-income individuals or first-time home buyers), directing them to optimized landing pages.

Tactic: Local SEO and Google Business Profile

- **Why:** Real estate is location-dependent, and businesses need to be visible in local search results.

- **Execution:** Optimize the website for local keywords like 'Best apartments in Bangalore/Bengaluru' or 'Houses for sale in Gurgaon/Gurugram'. Having an active Google Business Profile ensures the company appears in local map searches, and positive reviews can build trust.

- **Example:** A local real estate developer in Mumbai might optimize for 'Luxury flats in South Mumbai' and encourage satisfied clients to leave reviews on Google.

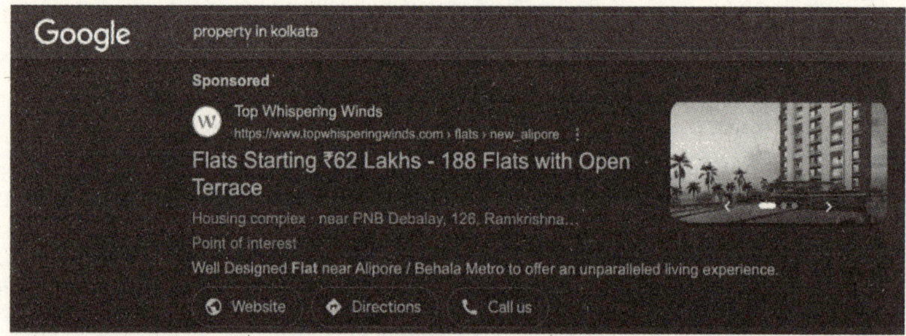

Image source: Google search results

14.2 E-Commerce: Focus on Conversion Optimization and Retargeting

Tactic: Conversion Rate Optimization (CRO)

- **Why:** E-commerce businesses depend on driving online purchases. Improving website usability and conversion rates directly impacts revenue.

- **Execution:** Regular A/B testing of website elements (e.g., product page layouts, CTA buttons) can increase conversion rates. E-commerce stores often use tools like Optimizely to optimize their checkout process, or recommend related products.

- **Example:** A fashion retailer might test different headlines like '20% Off Summer Collection' versus 'Limited Time Offer: Shop Now' to see which drives more conversions.

Tactic: Retargeting Ads

- **Why:** Retargeting is essential for e-commerce, where cart abandonment rates are high.

- **Execution:** Implement retargeting campaigns using platforms like Google Ads or Meta Ads to show personalized ads to users who have visited the website but didn't complete a purchase.

- **Example:** An online electronics store retargets visitors who viewed a laptop but didn't buy it, offering a special discount via retargeted Facebook ads.

Source: Behera[2]

14.3 Fashion: Focus on Influencer and Social Media Marketing

- **Tactic**: Collaborations with influencers, user-generated content (UGC), and Meta ads.

- **Nuance**: In the competitive fashion industry, visually compelling content that showcases trends and styles on real people is crucial. Influencers help create an aspirational brand image and encourage followers to make purchases through authentic reviews.

Source: Flipkart[3]

The 'Good Bug x HRX' collaboration is a perfect example of getting celebrities and influencers—who represent a certain niche industry—for your marketing if it matches your niche

- **Example**: A sustainable fashion start-up may partner with eco-conscious influencers to create Instagram Stories and Reels, showing the brand's unique value and encouraging immediate engagement.

14.4 B2B SaaS: Focus on Lead Nurturing and Inbound Marketing

Tactic: Lead Nurturing with Email Marketing

- **Why:** In B2B SaaS, the buying cycle is often longer, and leads require nurturing before making a purchase decision.

- **Execution:** Develop automated email sequences that educate potential customers over time. Emails may include case studies, product demos, and white papers to guide prospects through the buyer's journey.

- **Example:** A SaaS company offering project management software sends automated emails to leads who downloaded an e-book, following up with a free trial offer or personalized demo invitation.

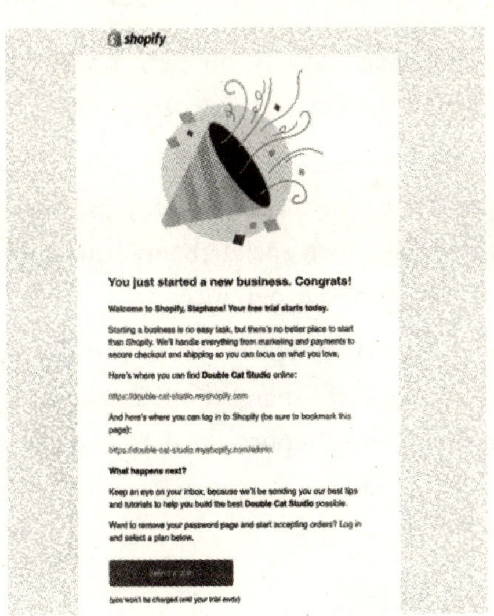

Image source: Stripo.email[4]

Tactic: Inbound Marketing via SEO and Blogging

- **Why:** SaaS companies need to attract leads through helpful content that positions them as experts in their niche.

- **Execution:** A content strategy focused on SEO, including blogs, case studies, and e-books targeting pain points of their audience (e.g., 'How to improve team collaboration' or 'Top tools for remote work').

- **Example:** A SaaS company specializing in HR software may create content on 'Best practices for employee engagement', driving organic traffic and positioning itself as a thought leader.

14.5 Hospitality: Focus on Social Proof and Visual Marketing

Tactic: Social Proof through User-Generated Content

- **Why:** Travelers rely heavily on peer reviews and social proof when choosing hotels or travel experiences.

- **Execution:** Encourage customers to post photos and reviews on social media using branded hashtags. Share user-generated content across your own social channels to build credibility and showcase real customer experiences.

- **Example:** A luxury hotel may run an Instagram campaign encouraging guests to share their staycation photos using a specific hashtag, then repost the best images on their official account.

Image source: Lemontree Hotels' Instagram[5]

Tactic: Visual Content, Influencer Collaborations and Storytelling

- **Why:** Hospitality businesses need to create a sense of experience and a strong desire to visit the destination through visual marketing.

- **Execution:** Use high-quality photos and videos showcasing the hotel, restaurant, or travel destination on Instagram, YouTube, or Pinterest. Partner with travel influencers to reach a larger audience and leverage their followers' trust.

- **Example:** A beach resort partners with a travel blogger to create a series of YouTube vlogs highlighting the resort's amenities, local attractions, and luxury experiences, driving bookings.

14.6 Education and E-Learning: Value-Driven Content and Webinars

Tactic: Free Resources, Webinars, and Targeted LinkedIn Ads

- **Nuance**: Educational platforms should focus on showcasing the value of their courses by offering sample classes, free resources, or webinars. LinkedIn targeting and search ads also help reach professionals and students looking to upskill.

- **Example:** An edtech company might offer free introductory sessions for popular courses to attract sign-ups, allowing potential customers to experience the learning platform first-hand.

Key Takeaway

Tailoring tactics to each sector's unique characteristics and customer expectations not only helps reach the right audience, but also strengthens the brand's overall marketing effectiveness.

Digital marketing tactics must be customized based on the specific goals, customer journey, and industry dynamics. As cited earlier, while real estate might focus on lead generation and local SEO, e-commerce needs to prioritize retargeting and conversion optimization. Healthcare relies on educational content, while B2B SaaS emphasizes lead nurturing. Tailoring these tactics ensures that the unique needs and challenges of each sector are met effectively, leading to better results and higher ROI.

Now that you've got a solid understanding of the strategies to grow beyond average, the next big question hits home: Who's going to make it all happen? As a founder or business owner, you've probably debated whether to hire an in-house team that knows your brand inside out or partner with an agency that brings specialized skills and fresh perspectives.

It's about trust, efficiency, budget and finding the right fit for your vision. In the next chapter, we'll unpack the real challenges and rewards of both options, helping you decide which path makes the most sense for you and your business. Because at the end of the day, the right team can make all the difference.

SECTION III

Slay the Game

15

Metrics Matter: Analyse, Monitor, and Optimize

DID YOU KNOW YOU CAN TRACK SOMETHING LIKE 'scroll depth'—that is, how far people are scrolling—on your website? Cool, right?

Now you're left sitting there with this shiny new piece of info, thinking, 'Great... now what do I do with it? Where can I use this?'

That's the thing about metrics—they sound impressive, but every time you learn a new one, it's like adding another puzzle piece without even knowing what the big picture looks like.

Most start-up founders and business owners either don't focus on metrics, or stick to tracking the basics—likes, comments, shares—without analysing, because honestly, that's what we hear about the most.

Analysing the metrics plays a crucial role in determining whether a particular marketing strategy is even working, or it's just money down the drain. There's a whole world of metrics out there you *could* be tracking—but without knowing what to track and where to use it inside your marketing strategy, it can be overwhelming. It's like being handed a map without knowing the destination. That's the problem. 'We're chasing surface-level data without a clear plan, hoping it somehow connects, instead of focusing on the metrics that actually drive results.'[1]

Metrics act as a spotlight, revealing what's working and what's not, so you can make impactful adjustments before it's late. It's these unnoticed details that often hold the key to significant growth.

Monitoring and optimizing digital marketing efforts are essential for ensuring the success of a campaign. Continuous tracking, analysing performance data, and making adjustments based on insights are crucial to improving ROI.

Data-driven Retargeting for Home furniture

Imagine a furniture retailer, HomeCraft, which heavily invests in social media ads to promote its custom, eco-friendly furniture. It runs ads showcasing its pieces across Instagram and Facebook, hoping to reach design-conscious buyers. Despite spending significantly, HomeCraft sees only a slight increase in online engagement and minimal sales conversions, which it attributes to its targeting or the quality of its ads.

However, HomeCraft does not actively *analyse* or *monitor* key metrics, such as click-through rate (CTR), conversion rate, cost per acquisition (CPA), or customer engagement patterns. It isn't using tracking pixels or integrating Google Analytics to gather insights on how users interact with its website after clicking on the ads. Here's the result.

1. **Misaligned targeting**: Without examining the analytics, HomeCraft is unaware that a large portion of its traffic comes from younger users interested in decor tips rather than actual buyers. It's targeting the wrong audience segment, resulting in low conversions and wasted ad spend.

2. **Content effectiveness**: It continues running the same ad creatives for months, assuming they're visually appealing. But

without A/B testing or monitoring CTRs, HomeCraft misses the fact that certain images and headlines perform far better than others, leading to an underwhelming engagement rate.

3. **Missed opportunities for retargeting**: It isn't using retargeting ads to re-engage visitors who left its website without making a purchase. Without monitoring, it misses opportunities to show ads to warm leads (people who browsed or added items to the cart), potentially increasing its conversion rate.

4. **Overspending**: Without tracking CPA, HomeCraft can't identify which ads are giving it the highest ROI. As a result, it overspends on underperforming ads, draining its marketing budget without clear benefits.

Outcome: After months of investment, HomeCraft realizes it's been burning through its budget with minimal results. By not analysing and optimizing campaigns, it wastes money on poorly performing ads, reaches the wrong audience, and fails to capitalize on potential sales. A more data-driven approach could have shown it the value of retargeting ads, refining its targeting and rotating high-performing content. This would have helped HomeCraft maximize its ad spend, improve conversions, and ultimately drive higher sales.

Do you remember the difference between studying the entire year versus studying for your exams a night before? It's the same here. Early insights help you spot what's not working before you've poured in too much time, money, or resources. Especially for start-ups and business owners, metrics aren't just numbers—they're the difference between scaling up or sinking.

Let us now see how to get it done.

Image source: Author's illustration

Below are some practical examples of how companies can monitor and optimize their digital marketing efforts.

15.1 Monitoring Paid Advertising Campaigns: Google Ads Example

Scenario: A SaaS start-up is running a Google Ads campaign to drive sign-ups for its free trial.

Monitoring Efforts

- The company regularly tracks key metrics such as cost-per-click (CPC), click-through rate (CTR), and conversion rate using Google Analytics and Google Ads Dashboard.

- They use A/B testing on ad copy to identify which versions of the ads are leading to higher conversion rates.

Optimization

- After two weeks of monitoring, the start-up notices that one ad group has a high CTR but a low conversion rate, indicating that while the ad is attractive, it isn't targeting the right audience.

- Based on this, they adjust their targeting criteria by refining keywords and excluding non-relevant terms to focus on their ideal customer base.

- They also tweak the landing page by simplifying the sign-up process, which ultimately improves the conversion rate.

In the daily grind, especially when we're juggling multiple roles, it's easy to overlook the small details. But these seemingly minor tweaks—like refining targeting or simplifying a process—can lead to game-changing results.

15.2 Optimizing Social Media Marketing: Facebook Ads for E-commerce

Scenario: An e-commerce business sells handmade jewellery and is running a Facebook Ads campaign to promote a new product line.

Monitoring Efforts

- The business monitors metrics such as impressions, engagement, and cost per acquisition (CPA) through the Facebook Ads Manager.

- They set up Pixel Tracking to follow customer behaviour after clicking on the ad and visiting their website.

Optimization

- After a few days of running the ads, they notice that while the ad is getting a lot of clicks, the bounce rate is high on the product page.

- The team uses heat maps to analyse user behaviour and realizes that the page load time is too slow.

- They optimize the product page for faster load times, which reduces the bounce rate and increases the number of purchases.

- Additionally, based on demographics data, they shift their ad targeting from broad age groups to specific segments (e.g., 25–34-year-old women), which leads to a lower CPA and a higher ROAS.

While observing business owners over the years, I've noticed how often we blame the product or content when results fall short. But without tracking metrics, crucial details—like slow page load times—get completely overlooked. Simple tools can pinpoint these hidden issues, showing us that sometimes, the fix isn't what we expect. Analysing these metrics helps us focus on the right problems before they derail growth.

15.3 SEO Monitoring and Optimization: Blogging for Lead Generation

Scenario: A B2B tech start-up is using a content marketing strategy by publishing blog posts to generate leads. The main goal is to improve their website's ranking on search engines and attract organic traffic.

Monitoring Efforts

- The team uses Google Search Console and SEMrush to monitor their keyword rankings, track traffic to their blog posts, and assess backlink growth.

- They monitor key performance indicators (KPIs) like organic traffic, time on page, and bounce rates.

Optimization

- Over time, they notice that a few blog posts are ranking well but are not converting visitors into leads.

- To address this, they optimize the calls-to-action (CTAs) on these pages by making them more prominent and aligning them with the reader's intent (e.g., offering a free eBook download in exchange for an email).

- Additionally, they update outdated content by incorporating more relevant keywords, adding internal links to related content, and using schema markup to improve search engine visibility.

- These optimizations lead to higher organic search rankings and increased lead generation.

With keyword stuffing being one of the most common—yet misguided—pieces of advice for organic SEO ranking, many businesses focus on cramming as many keywords as possible into their content, which in turn causes more harm than good.

What really matters is how natural and relevant those keywords are, alongside factors like user engagement and content quality. Metrics like bounce rate, average session duration, and conversion rates are what truly reveal the effectiveness of your SEO efforts and guide you toward real, long-term success.

15.4 Email Marketing Monitoring and Optimization: Personalized Campaigns

Scenario: An online education platform is running an email marketing campaign to increase course enrolments.

Monitoring Efforts

- The team tracks metrics like open rates, click-through rates, and unsubscribe rates using an email marketing tool like Mailchimp.

- They segment their email list based on user behaviour, such as whether the recipient has previously enrolled in a course or is a first-time visitor.

Optimization

- After monitoring, they find that their open rates are low for a specific segment of users who haven't engaged with the platform recently.

- To re-engage this audience, they create a personalized email campaign offering a discount on courses they've previously shown interest in, and use A/B testing to try different subject lines.

- By adding a sense of urgency (e.g., limited-time offer) and improving personalization, they see a 20 per cent increase in open rates and a subsequent rise in course enrolments.

Doesn't matter the industry, we observe several cases of strategies relying on guessing games, or copying what works for others in the industry, thinking it's the safest bet. But what works for one business may completely miss the mark for yours. Testing allows you to move beyond assumptions, uncover what truly resonates with your audience, and make data-backed decisions.

15.5 Monitoring and Optimizing Influencer Marketing: Instagram Campaign

Scenario: A fashion start-up partners with an Instagram influencer to promote its new clothing line.

Monitoring Efforts

- The company uses tools like Sprout Social and HypeAuditor to track influencer campaign metrics, such as engagement rate, follower growth, and sales driven from influencer posts.

- They track unique referral links provided to the influencer to see exactly how many conversions were generated from the partnership.

Optimization

- After reviewing the performance data, they notice that while engagement is high, the actual sales conversion is low.

- They adjust the campaign by providing the influencer with a discount code to share with their audience, making it easier to track purchases, and incentivizing users to convert.

- Additionally, they ask the influencer to create more engaging behind-the-scenes content (e.g., styling tips) to build a deeper connection with their audience, which leads to increased conversions.

A huge mistake many business owners make with influencer campaigns is blindly trusting follower counts, which can often be inflated or fake. This leads to sky high marketing charges with minimal results, if any. But when you dive deeper into the metrics—looking at engagement rates, audience demographics, and authenticity—you uncover the real value an influencer can bring, making your investment work harder for you.

15.6 Key Metrics

Here are the key digital marketing metrics presented in structured tables for clarity:

Table 1: Traffic Metrics

Metric	Definition	Why It Matters	Formula
Website Traffic	Total visitors to your website	Tracks visibility and reach	N/A
Traffic Sources	Breakdown by channel (organic, paid, etc.)	Identifies high-performing channels	N/A
Click-Through Rate (CTR)	% of users who clicked an ad/link	Measures ad and link effectiveness	(Clicks / impressions) x 100
Bounce Rate	% leaving after viewing one page	Indicates landing page or UX issues	(Single-page sessions / Total sessions) x 100
Average Session Duration	Time users spend on the site	Measures engagement	Total duration of sessions / Total sessions

Table 2: Conversion Metrics

Metric	Definition	Why It Matters	Formula
Conversion Rate	% completing desired actions (e.g., purchase, sign-up)	Tracks how well traffic converts	(Conversions / Total visitors) x 100
Cost-Per-Conversion (CPC)	Average cost per conversion	Tracks cost-efficiency	Total ad spend / Conversions
Cost-Per-Acquisition (CPA)	Cost to acquire one customer	Measures profitability of campaigns	Total Ad spend / New customers

Metric	Definition	Why It Matters	Formula
Lead-to-Customer Ratio	% of leads that become customers	Indicates nurturing effectiveness	(Customers / Leads) x 100

Table 3: Revenue Metrics

Metric	Definition	Why It Matters	Formula
Return on Ad Spend (ROAS)	Revenue earned per dollar spent on ads	Measures profitability of ad campaigns	Revenue from ads / Ad spend
Customer Lifetime Value (CLV)	Total revenue from a customer over time	Helps optimize acquisition spending	Varies
Average Order Value (AOV)	Average revenue per order	Tracks upselling and cross-selling efforts	Total revenue / Total orders

Table 4: Engagement Metrics

Metric	Definition	Why It Matters	Formula
Engagement Rate	% of users engaging with your content	Indicates content relevance	(Engagements / Impressions) x 100
Social Media Reach	Number of unique users who saw your content	Measures brand awareness	N/A
Video View Rate	% of users who viewed a video	Evaluates video content appeal	(Video views / Impressions) x 100

Metric	Definition	Why It Matters	Formula
Email Open Rate	% of recipients who opened an email	Tracks email subject line effectiveness	(Emails opened / Emails sent) x 100
Email Click Rate	% of recipients clicking on a link in email	Measures email content engagement	(Clicks / Emails delivered) x 100

Table 5: Paid Advertising Metrics

Metric	Definition	Why It Matters	Formula
Cost Per Click (CPC)	Cost per click on an ad	Tracks cost-efficiency of campaigns	Total ad spend / Clicks
Impressions	Total times an ad is shown	Measures reach of ads	N/A
Quality Score	Google Ads relevance and quality rating	Affects CPC and ad rankings	Google algorithm
Ad Frequency	Average times an ad is shown to a user	Helps prevent ad fatigue	Impressions / Unique users

Table 6: Retargeting and Tracking Metrics

Metric	Definition	Why It Matters	Formula
Pixel Tracking	Tracks user activity for retargeting	Creates targeted campaigns	N/A
Retargeting CTR	Engagement on retargeted ads	Indicates retargeting effectiveness	(Clicks / Impressions) x 100

Metric	Definition	Why It Matters	Formula
Customer Retention Rate	% of customers retained over a period	Measures loyalty	(Customers End–New customers) / Customers start x 100

Table 7: SEO and Content Metrics

Metric	Definition	Why it Matters	Formula
Organic Traffic	Visitors from search engines	Tracks SEO performance	N/A
Keyword Rankings	Position of targeted keywords	Measures search visibility	N/A
Backlinks	Quality and quantity of inbound links	Affects domain authority and rankings	N/A
Pages per Session	Average pages viewed per session	Reflects content engagement	Total page views / Sessions

Table 8: ROI Metrics

Metric	Definition	Why It Matters	Formula
Marketing ROI	Overall profitability of marketing campaigns	Tracks ROI of efforts	(Revenue – Marketing cost) / Marketing cost x 100
Cost Per Lead (CPL)	Average cost to generate a lead	Measures lead generation efficiency	Total ad spend / Leads generated

Key Takeaways

- ✓ **Continuous monitoring:** Regularly track performance metrics such as CTR, conversion rates, CPA, and ROAS using analytics tools.

- ✓ **A/B testing:** Run experiments on ad copy, landing pages, and CTAs to identify what resonates best with your target audience.

- ✓ **Data-driven optimization:** Use insights gained from tracking to make necessary adjustments, such as improving page load times, tweaking audience targeting, or adjusting budgets.

- ✓ **Real-time adjustments:** Digital marketing allows for real-time monitoring, so you can quickly pivot campaigns that aren't performing as expected.

- ✓ **Automation and personalization:** Use email marketing tools to automate personalized follow-ups, and optimize campaign timing to increase engagement and conversions.

Effective monitoring and optimization ensure that digital marketing efforts are not just set and forgotten, but continuously refined to achieve the best possible results.

It's about tracking the metrics, making adjustments early, and letting go of what's not working. By doubling down on what's actually driving results, you turn doubts into a well-thought-out strategy for growth. It's not about guessing—it's about testing, learning, and refining your way to success.

16

Automate to Elevate: Automation for Growth

'IF IT'S AUTOMATED, WILL IT STILL FEEL PERSONAL? WILL my customers sense it's not really *me*? Maybe that's why I haven't tapped into them yet—it's a mix of being overwhelmed, and this lingering fear of losing the human touch my business is built on.' This is what one of my industry friends said on a random Friday evening while we were talking about using Artificial Intelligence (AI) and automations for his super-cool new venture. I knew it was an awesome idea from the day he shared it two years back.

But so much has changed since then. Having an awesome idea isn't enough to connect with millions of awesome people who would benefit from it.

Can you recall the days when social media was just a way to connect with friends? Platforms like Facebook and Twitter were simple, basic—mainly a digital space for sharing updates. Then came the rise of paid ads, influencer marketing, and algorithms that gradually reshaped the entire experience.

Suddenly, engagement wasn't just about sharing; it was about reaching the right audience, paying for visibility, and mastering the shifting landscape of algorithms. Now, it's no longer just about having a presence online; it's about how much smarter, faster, and more targeted your strategy can be.

Just like the evolution of social media, AI and automation are shaking up digital marketing. At first, there's scepticism—will it work? But just like with social media, there's no going back. Embracing these tools isn't a choice anymore; it's a necessity to stay ahead.

So, let's talk about scaling your business with automations in this chapter; why you need it, and how you can make the best use of it minus being overwhelmed.

'Less than 1 per cent of data in businesses is analysed and turned into benefits,' according to SAP.[1]

Scaling and automation are critical aspects of digital marketing for start-ups aiming to grow without overwhelming their resources. By automating repetitive tasks and using scalable strategies, businesses can maximize efficiency and reach more customers.

Let's take an in-depth insight into CityStay Boutique Hotels as an example.

Automating for Relevance in a Hotel Business

CityStay Boutique Hotels operates a chain of small, charming hotels in popular tourist areas across India. Known for its personalized service and unique decor, the company initially attracted steady bookings through word-of-mouth and organic social media presence. However, as the hospitality industry grew increasingly competitive, with larger hotel chains and online travel agencies investing in automation and digital marketing, CityStay struggled to keep pace due to its reliance on a manual marketing processes.

Challenges

1. **Manual booking management**: Without an automated booking platform, guests couldn't easily book online, leading to missed opportunities,

2. **No automated marketing campaigns**: They lacked a Customer Relationship Management (CRM) system to automate outreach, follow-ups, or targeted promotions. As a result, they missed valuable upsell opportunities, like offering returning guests discounts or personalized recommendations.

3. **Limited social media engagement and targeting**: They lacked the tools to analyse audience engagement and automate content scheduling or ad targeting. They could not analyse performance, reach wider audiences, and optimize ad spend.

Outcome

CityStay's inability to automate key areas of their digital marketing led to stagnation, with valuable staff time being used on repetitive tasks that could have been automated. Meanwhile, their lack of targeted outreach meant they missed chances to increase guest loyalty and retention. As competitors expanded their market share, their growth plateaued

Key Takeaway

This example demonstrates how failing to adopt automation in digital marketing can hinder growth, especially in a fast-paced industry like hospitality. Despite having a touch-base with tools like social media marketing, the lack of automation restricted the brand from reaping its benefits.

Let us see some practical examples of scaling and automation in digital marketing.

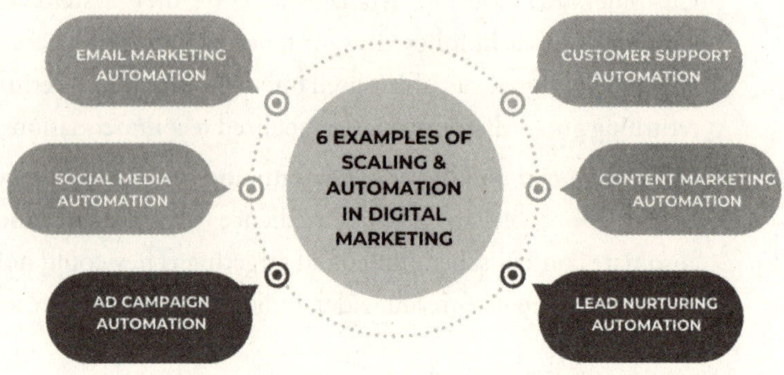

Image source: Author's illustration

16.1 Email Marketing Automation: E-commerce Example

Scenario: An online retail store wants to engage its customers through personalized email marketing without manually sending each email.

Automation

The company uses an email marketing platform like Mailchimp or Klaviyo to set up automated email flows. Some of these flows include:

- o Welcome emails for new subscribers.

- o Abandoned cart emails to remind users to complete their purchase.

- o Post-purchase emails with product recommendations or asking for reviews.

- o Browse abandonment cart emails to leverage users who are browsing the store and convert them into customers.

Scaling

- Instead of sending individual emails, they automate the process based on user actions. For example, when a customer leaves an item in their cart, the system automatically sends a reminder email.

- This automation scales effortlessly as the customer base grows, allowing the business to continue offering personalized experiences without additional manual effort.

- If a product is subscription-based, regular emails are automated to send reminders to every customer based on their purchase date to continue retaining the customer.

- During any special occasion, such as a customer's birthday, special discounts and gift vouchers are sent through the automation set up to make them feel special while increasing brand loyalty and sales.

Results

- The automated abandoned cart emails result in a 15 per cent recovery rate for lost sales, and the post-purchase emails generate additional revenue through upselling.

- A lot of customers look forward to the special event discounts, such as their birthday, to make themselves feel special while continuing to be regular customers.

- As most people check their emails, email marketing acts as a constant brand reminder, keeping the brand in sight despite all the hustle bustle. The entire process can be automated for months to come, leaving a business owner's hands free.

16.2 Social Media Automation: Content Scheduling for SaaS Start-up

Scenario: A SaaS start-up uses social media to promote its software, but posting manually on multiple platforms (e.g., Facebook, LinkedIn, Twitter) is time-consuming.

Automation

- The company uses a tool like Hootsuite, Buffer, or Sprout Social to schedule posts across multiple social media platforms in advance.

- They automate social media engagement by setting up auto-responses for frequently asked questions through chatbots on Facebook Messenger and Instagram.

- They further automate their lead generation process using free downloads or exclusive content access. These leads then go through nurture workflows and follow-ups after form submissions or campaign interactions.

Scaling

- By scheduling content in bulk, the start-up can maintain a consistent posting schedule without needing to manage daily social media activities.

- As the company grows, they can add more platforms and content without significantly increasing workload, thanks to automated scheduling.

- Automated audience engagement messages via chatbots and lead generation helps the brand to have constant interaction with their potential customers and have a steady flow of leads.

Results

- This automated approach allows the start-up to focus on strategy while maintaining consistent engagement. Over time, they see an increase in social media followers and a 20 per cent growth in website traffic from social channels.

- The brand is able to establish their presence across multiple social media platforms, tweaking it as per the platform demands without having to spend extravagant resources. According to Forbes, businesses that adopt an omnichannel strategy retain 89 per cent of their customers, compared to just 33 per cent for companies without such a strategy. **source**

16.3 Ad Campaign Automation: Google Ads for Lead Generation

Scenario: A real estate business uses Google Ads to generate leads for its high-end residential properties. Managing multiple ad campaigns manually is resource-intensive.

Automation

- The business sets up smart bidding on Google Ads, allowing the platform to automatically adjust bids based on the likelihood of conversion. They also use automated rules to pause underperforming ads or adjust budgets during peak hours.

- Google Ads' responsive search ads dynamically create multiple versions of the ad, combining different headlines and descriptions to maximize performance without needing manual intervention.

- Audience targeting automations support Google Ads to analyse user behaviour and demographics using tools like Customer Match and Similar Audiences. This process helps to maximize engagement and ad relevance.

Scaling

- As the business expands to different cities, they can easily scale their Google ads by duplicating campaigns and adjusting location settings. The automation handles bid adjustments, keyword management, and ad rotation across all cities.

- Automating the process to evaluate ads and pause the ones not working allows the brands to divert their resources into ads that are generating higher ROI without having to manually evaluate that constantly.

Results

- Automation leads to a 25 per cent reduction in cost per lead (CPL) while increasing the number of qualified leads generated by 30 per cent.

- Automating repetitive tasks like bid adjustments, keyword management, and analysing ads allow marketers to focus their time on strategy and creative improvements, making them time-efficient.

16.4 Customer Support Automation: Chatbots for an Online Marketplace

Scenario: An online marketplace experiences high volumes of customer inquiries, particularly around product availability, shipping times, and return policies.

Automation

- The marketplace integrates a chatbot on its website, using a tool like Zendesk, Intercom, or Drift. The chatbot can answer frequently asked questions (FAQs), guide customers through the purchase process, and even handle simple order inquiries.

- Customized chatbots further help potential customers with their shopping recommendations, as per their past purchases, style and vibe preferences. This makes the experience highly customized, boosting cross-selling and upselling opportunities.

Scaling

- As the marketplace grows and experiences more traffic, the chatbot handles an increasing number of customer queries without needing additional customer support staff.

- The system can escalate more complex issues to human agents when necessary, ensuring a seamless customer experience while managing high volumes of inquiries.

- With AI-driven insights, these chatbots can upsell and cross-sell based on the user's past purchase history, helping the brand to scale-up their sales, retain further customers and establish further brand loyalty.

Results

- The chatbot resolves 60 per cent of customer inquiries without human intervention, allowing the company to scale customer service operations without increasing costs.

- Based on personalized recommendations, 49 per cent of consumers are willing to make spontaneous purchases. This speaks volumes about just how effective these personalized automated chatbots are. **source**

16.5 Lead-Nurturing Automation: CRM for a B2B Tech Start-up

Scenario: A B2B tech start-up generates leads through webinars and white paper downloads, but struggles to follow-up with leads manually.

Automation

- They implement a Customer Relationship Management (CRM) system like HubSpot or Salesforce, which automates lead nurturing through a series of drip email campaigns.

- The CRM triggers emails based on user actions (e.g., attending a webinar, downloading a white paper), moving leads through the sales funnel.

- They further use WhatsApp Business API CRM for webinars by enabling automated registration, reminders, and follow-ups. This increases attendee engagement through personalized messages, updates, and resource-sharing, ensuring a seamless participant experience while reducing manual workload.

Scaling

- As the number of leads grows, the CRM system manages the lead flow without the need for manual follow-ups. The system can score leads based on engagement, helping the sales team prioritize high-value prospects.

- Automation ensures that leads receive personalized content based on their behaviour, while the sales team focuses on closing deals with high-potential clients.

- This increases customer conversion and retention as the leads are constantly followed up, reminding them of the value, incentives and time-sensitive offers.

Results

- The automated lead nurturing sequence increases lead conversion by 20 per cent, allowing the start-up to handle a larger pipeline without additional sales staff.

- The CRM systems improve response times by up to 74 per cent, enabling seminar organizers to follow-up quickly with attendees, reducing the risk of losing potential conversions due to delays

- The automated CRM system creates personalized customer experiences, resulting in a 112 per cent increase in customer satisfaction, allowing the brand to tailor communication and offers based on attendee preferences and behaviours.

Key Takeaways

- **Email automation:** Automating email sequences based on user behaviour ensures personalized communication without manual effort. Tools like Mailchimp can scale as the subscriber base grows.

- **Social media automation:** Scheduling posts and automating engagement with tools like Hootsuite or Buffer helps manage multiple social platforms efficiently.

- **Ad automation:** Smart bidding and automated ad adjustments in platforms like Google Ads ensure optimal performance and scalability as marketing budgets increase.

- **Customer support automation:** Chatbots handle routine inquiries, freeing up human agents for complex issues, enabling customer support to scale with demand.

- **Content automation:** Tools like WordPress and Zapier ensure consistent content distribution, while CRMs automate lead nurturing, allowing for seamless scalability.

By implementing such examples, start-ups can focus on growth while ensuring their digital marketing efforts remain efficient and scalable.

As Bill Gates said, 'Automation applied to an inefficient operation will magnify the inefficiency.'[2]

In order to truly thrive in a fast-paced digital landscape, you need to adapt quickly and efficiently. In the next chapter, we'll dive into the power of AI—how to respond, pivot, and adjust in real time without losing momentum. Get ready to discover how flexibility, rapid iteration, and continuous feedback can transform your approach, ensuring you stay ahead of the curve in an ever-changing market.

17

AI: The Final Frontier

ARTIFICIAL INTELLIGENCE IS RESHAPING MARKETING IN ways most businesses still don't fully understand. I've seen countless brands either underutilize it with basic automations, or get lost in a sea of tools, hoping technology alone will fix their marketing. But here's the truth—you won't see results from AI just because it's 'trendy'; you'll see results when you make it an extension of your strategy.

Artificial Intelligence can't replace smart marketing, but it can enhance it. When you use it right, it becomes your partner—accelerating tasks, sharpening insights, and helping you scale creativity.

Look at how Myntra uses AI with its My Stylist feature. The tool analyses browsing behaviour, purchase history, and even uploaded images to suggest complete outfits tailored to individual preferences. This isn't just automation—it's personalization at scale, designed to enhance the customer experience and drive sales more effectively.

But that is Myntra—a well-established e-commerce giant. Most businesses don't know how to leverage AI for results. They either stop at basic chat assistants, or stack tools without a clear plan. I've worked with brands where AI felt more like a distraction than a solution—until we got intentional with how it was used.

I want you to leave this chapter with clarity. Not vague ideas or random tools, but a clear understanding of how AI fits into your marketing.

In the context of marketing, every effective AI tool falls into two core categories:

1.   For strategy and ideation (generative AI assistants)
2.   For execution (task-specific automation tools)

It is very important to know which tool is useful in which particular area of marketing. Always remember—the tool is only as effective as the individual using it.

Let me break down both these categories and look at the use cases where AI tools come in handy.

17.1 AI Tools for Strategy and Planning

These tools focus on helping you think bigger, plan smarter, and generate creative ideas more efficiently. Large language models (LLMs) like ChatGPT, Claude, and Gemini can assist with brainstorming campaigns, generating content ideas, and drafting copy. They help you explore creative angles and refine messaging strategies, acting as a strategic partner in the early stages of marketing planning.

For example, you can use an AI assistant to generate multiple campaign ideas, suggest variations for Instagram captions, or draft an ad script. These tools don't just save time—they offer fresh perspectives based on vast datasets, helping you break creative blocks and think more clearly.

My team consistently uses LLM tools for early stage campaign planning, where they've helped break creative blocks and spark new ideas. When you guide them with the right prompts and business context, they act like a strategic brainstorming partner that speeds up the planning phase without sacrificing creativity.

Here are some of the most common use case scenarios in strategy and planning in digital marketing, and which AI tool is the most suitable in that particular scenario.

17.1.1 You're stuck and need fresh, creative campaign ideas

You need an AI that's great at brainstorming, generating new ideas, and helping you see creative angles you might not have thought of.

Best Tool/Model: **ChatGPT (OpenAI, GPT-4.5/5)**

Most marketers use ChatGPT wrong. They focus on basic tasks like writing social media posts. The real value lies in strategic planning. You'll get the most from it when:

- Developing campaign strategies from scratch
- Testing different marketing angles before execution
- Finding gaps in competitor approaches
- Creating content plans that connect with your audience
- Planning integrated campaigns across channels.

Example:

A start-up wants to launch a new eco-friendly water bottle. The marketing team uses ChatGPT to brainstorm campaign slogans, social media challenges, and influencer outreach ideas. Within an hour, they have a shortlist of creative concepts—one of which becomes their viral launch campaign.

17.1.2 You have lots of data (research, interviews, reports) but can't see the big picture or spot patterns.

You need an AI that excels at deep analysis, connecting details across long documents, and identifying hidden patterns.

Best Tool/Model: **Claude (Anthropic, Claude 3.5 Sonnet/ Opus)**

In marketing strategy, this matters more than you'd think. Most planning fails because we miss connections between different data points. Claude changes this. It helps you:

- Connect market research with campaign planning
- Turn customer feedback into strategic opportunities
- Develop content strategies that build momentum
- Spot patterns in campaign performance data.

Example:

A B2B company wants to reposition its software product. The team uploads competitor reports, customer interviews, and sales data into Claude. Claude finds that 'ease of integration' is a recurring customer concern—an insight the team had missed. They shift their messaging, resulting in a measurable uptick in demo requests.

17.1.3 You want to plan for the future—spotting trends, understanding new markets, and predicting what customers will want next

You need an AI that specializes in forecasting, trend analysis, and market segmentation—especially one that leverages real-time global data.

Best Tool/Model: **Gemini (Google, Gemini 1.5 Pro/Ultra)**

Most marketing tools look backward at data. Gemini helps you look forward. When planning your marketing strategy, it helps you:

- Identify market trends before they become obvious
- Understand shifting customer behaviours
- Map audience segments you haven't considered
- Plan region-specific marketing approaches.

17.1.4 You need the latest, most accurate information—fast. You want to know what's happening in our industry right now.

You need an AI that's a real-time research assistant, able to pull in up-to-date, source-cited information from across the web.

Best Tool/Model: **Perplexity (Perplexity AI, Claude 3.5 Sonnet integration)**

Most marketing tools give you surface-level answers. Perplexity helps you go deeper. When planning your marketing strategy, it helps you:

- Find nuanced insights that others miss
- Explore evolving customer questions in real time
- Uncover niche audience interests you haven't targeted
- Design content strategies tailored to specific markets

Example:

A retail brand wants to pitch a new "sustainable packaging" initiative. They use Perplexity to pull the latest industry reports, consumer sentiment data, and competitor moves—all with clickable sources. Their pitch is not only current, but also credible and well-documented.

17.1.5 You want to catch and capitalize on viral trends or public sentiment—right as they happen.

You need an AI that's plugged into live social data, able to spot trending topics, viral hashtags, and shifts in public mood instantly.

Best Tool/Model: **Grok AI (xAI, Grok-1.5/2)**

Most marketing tools give generic insights. Grok helps you think critically. When planning your marketing strategy, it helps you:

- Challenge assumptions before they limit your growth

- Reveal hidden patterns in customer behaviour
- Spot unconventional audience segments you haven't explored
- Develop creative, market-specific campaign ideas

Example:

A beauty brand notices a sudden spike in a new skincare trend on X (Twitter) using Grok. Within hours, they launch a themed campaign and influencer partnership, riding the wave for a 40 per cent jump in engagement and sales.

17.2 AI Tools for Execution

AI execution tools simplify how you bring marketing ideas to life, helping you move faster without compromising on quality. They assist with everything from creating visuals and writing copy to automating campaign optimization and audience personalization, handling tasks that often drain time and resources.

For instance, Canva's Magic Design generates branded templates in seconds, while InVideo transforms scripts into polished Reels and ads with minimal effort. Tools like Jasper and Copy.ai can generate entire email sequences tailored to audience segments, while platforms such as Adzooma can analyse your ad performance and automatically adjust targeting, budgets, and messaging for better results.

The real power is how these tools streamline your workflow. I've seen brands cut down production timelines from weeks to days using AI-driven automation, while still maintaining creative control. When combined with a focused strategy, they help you scale campaigns, reduce manual effort, and stay consistent across all channels.

Here's a list of AI tools for execution and operations across various digital marketing departments (Note: Some tools here are not purely 'AI tools' but platforms with AI-powered features that enhance their core functionality).

17.2.1 SEO

Artificial Intelligence-powered SEO tools help you optimize content for search engines more effectively than traditional methods. These tools analyse top-ranking pages, understand search intent, and guide your content creation.

Most Popular

- **Semrush**: AI-powered suite for keyword research, SEO audits, and competitive analysis.

- **Frase**: AI content optimizer for improving search rankings based on SERP analysis.

- **MarketMuse**: AI-driven platform for mapping content gaps and building authority.

- **Surfer**: Real-time SERP analyzer and content scoring for on-page SEO.

Other Options

- Clearscope: Previously strong, but now surpassed by newer AI-driven SEO tools.

- SEO.ai: Fast-growing platform for AI-powered SEO content creation and optimization.

17.2.2 Written Content Creation

Content creation tools powered by AI help you draft high-quality text efficiently, from blog posts and email campaigns to social media captions and product descriptions. These tools enhance your writing process while ensuring consistency and creativity.

Most Popular

- **Copy.ai**: AI writing assistant for blog posts, emails, and marketing copy.

- **Jasper**: Advanced AI content generator with brand voice and workflow features.
- **Copysmith**: AI-powered copywriting for product descriptions and collaboration.

Other Options

- **BlogFox**: Less prominent and limited adoption in 2025.
- **Writesonic**: Popular for high-quality, long-form, and marketing content.

17.2.3 Video Creation

Video creation tools powered by AI simplify the process of producing professional, engaging videos by leveraging features like customizable templates, AI-generated avatars, automated editing, and advanced visual effects.

Most Popular

- **InVideo**: AI-powered video editor with templates and automated media selection.
- **Synthesia**: Leading AI video platform with avatars and multilingual voiceovers.
- **Descript**: Edit video/audio by editing text, with AI-powered features.
- **RunwayML**: Generative AI tools for creative video editing and special effects.

Other Options

- **Haiper**: Niche; more mainstream and advanced tools are now available.
- **HeyGen**: Fast-growing for realistic AI avatars and voice cloning.

- **Google Veo 2**: High-resolution, cinematic AI video generation.
- **Hailou AI**: New AI video tool for rapid, automated video creation with advanced effects.
- **Dreamia**: Innovative platform for AI-driven video storytelling and generative visuals.

17.2.4 Social Media Marketing

Artificial Intelligence tools for social media marketing help you create impactful content, streamline post scheduling, analyse performance metrics, and enhance visuals. They empower you to understand your audience better, refine your strategy, and engage more effectively.

Most Popular

- **Ocoya**: AI-driven platform for content creation and post scheduling.
- **Rival IQ**: Social analytics and competitor benchmarking.
- **Canva**: Magic Studio for AI-powered design and copy.
- **Lately AI**: AI repurposing of long-form content for social media posts.
- **LetsEnhance**: AI image upscaling and enhancement.

Other Options

- **Hootsuite Insights:** AI analytics and social management.
- **FeedHive:** AI-optimized social scheduling and engagement.
- **Sprout Social:** AI-powered audience insights and engagement.17.2.5 Ad Management

17.2.5 Ad Management

Ad management tools driven by AI automate and enhance various aspects of advertising campaigns, including audience targeting, budget allocation, creative optimization, and performance analysis, enabling you to achieve better results with greater efficiency.

Most Popular

- **Albert by Zoomd**: Autonomous ad optimization across channels.
- **Trapica**: AI-powered audience targeting and campaign adaptation.
- **Metadata**: Automated paid campaign management with ABM focus.
- **Revealbot**: Multi-platform ad automation and performance rules.

Other Options

- **Pathmatics**: More for ad intelligence, less for automation.
- **AdCreative.ai**: AI-generated ad creatives for all major platforms..

17.2.6 Email Marketing

Email marketing tools powered by AI assist in crafting personalized content, automating campaign workflows, and analysing engagement metrics, enabling you to connect more effectively with your audience and optimize your email strategies.

Most Popular

- **ActiveCampaign**: AI-driven automation, personalization, and insights.
- **Mailchimp**: AI-powered analytics and content suggestions.
- **Seventh Sense**: AI send-time optimization for higher engagement.

Other Options

- **Mailsplash**: Less prominent.

- **EverMail AI**: Not widely recognized.

- **Klaviyo**: Leading for AI-powered segmentation and personalization.

- **GetResponse**: AI-optimized email marketing and automation.

17.2.7 Customer Engagement

Customer engagement tools powered by AI facilitate personalized interactions, automate responses, and provide insights into customer behaviour, enabling you to build stronger relationships and improve satisfaction.

Most Popular

- **Gorgias**: AI-enhanced e-commerce customer support.

- **Intercom**: AI-first customer service with Fin AI Agent.

- **Tidio**: Live chat and AI chatbot automation.

Other Options

- **Zendesk AI**: AI customer service and ticket management.

- **Freshdesk Freddy AI**: AI-powered support and workflow automation.

17.2.8 Brand Monitoring

Brand monitoring tools powered by AI enable you to track mentions, analyse sentiment, and monitor trends across various platforms, providing valuable insights to manage your brand's reputation effectively.

Most Popular

- **Mentionlytics**: Social listening and brand monitoring.
- **NewsWhip**: Real-time media and trend monitoring.
- **Keyhole**: Social media analytics and hashtag tracking.

Other Options

- **Brandwatch Consumer Research**: AI sentiment and trend analysis.
- **Profound**: Deep AI search tracking and enterprise monitoring.
- **ZipTie**: Monitors brand visibility in AI search engines.
- **Gumshoe AI**: Persona-based audience and visibility insights.

17.2.9 Data Analytics

Data analytics tools powered by AI assist in collecting, processing, and interpreting complex datasets, providing actionable insights to inform strategic decisions and optimize business performance.

Most Popular

- **Google Analytics 4**: Industry standard for web and campaign analytics.
- **Pendo**: Product analytics and user behaviour tracking.
- **Sisense**: Business intelligence and analytics platform.

Other Options

- **InsightSquared**: Less prominent in 2025.
- **Airtable AI**: AI-native analytics and workflow automation.
- **Brandwatch**: Advanced consumer intelligence and social listening.

17.2.10 Project Management

Project management tools powered by AI streamline workflows, automate routine tasks, and provide intelligent insights, enabling teams to collaborate more effectively and complete projects efficiently.

Most Popular

- **ClickUp**: AI-powered project and workflow management.

Other Options

- **Leiga, Dart**: Not widely recognized.
- **Asana**: AI-powered task summaries and automation.
- **Zapier**: AI workflow automation connecting 1000+ tools.

17.3 Instances Where AI Is Revolutionizing Marketing

Let us see how some of the world's most innovative brands are using AI to revolutionize marketing. These real-world case studies showcase the power of AI to predict emerging trends before competitors, deliver hyper-personalized advertising at massive scale, engage customers with emotionally intelligent chatbots, and proactively reduce churn through predictive insights. Together, they demonstrate how AI is transforming marketing from a reactive, manual process into a data-driven, automated, and highly personalized strategy that drives real business impact.

17.3.1 Unilever Predicting the Rise of Vegan Ice Cream

What happened and when

In 2024, Unilever deployed AI-enabled freezers across its global network to monitor stock levels and sales trends in real time.[1]

Exactly what occurred

About 100,000 of their 3 million ice-cream freezers worldwide were equipped with smart sensors and cameras that used AI to analyse when products ran low.[2]

The AI also incorporated weather data to forecast consumer demand—for instance, a 1 °C rise in temperature could sharply boost sales. This AI not only anticipated stockouts but spotted emerging preferences, including rising demand for plant-based (vegan) alternatives.

Impact

Retail orders rose by up to 30 per cent, depending on the country (e.g., Denmark saw a 30 per cent increase). AI-generated insights enabled Unilever to launch vegan ice-cream lines faster than competitors, capitalizing on evolving consumer trends—effectively predicting the vegan wave before it peaked.

17.3.2. Cadbury's Shah Rukh Khan (SRK) Personalized Ad Campaign

What happened and when

During Diwali 2021, Cadbury Celebrations launched the 'Not Just a Cadbury Ad' campaign aimed at supporting local Indian businesses.[3]

Exactly what occurred

They used AI/ML (via Rephrase.ai) to generate hyper-personalized video ads featuring a digital avatar of SRK that spoke directly to a local store by name and location.

This ran across over 500 pin codes covering 2,000+ stores; users could also generate their own SRK videos via the campaign website.

Within two weeks, the campaign scaled from ~1,000 to ~20,000 personalized videos/day using voice-cloning and facial re-enactment tech.

Impact

It delivered 22 per cent higher view-through rates and 18 per cent higher CTR compared to standard ads.

Around 139,000 customized ads were created, with 105,000 users engaging on the website.

The campaign earned $1.5 M in unpaid PR and over 30 million ad views.

It won top creative recognition, including the Cannes Grand Prix for Creative Effectiveness in 2023.[4]

17.3.3 Bank of America's 'Erica': Sentiment-Aware Chatbot

What happened and when

Bank of America launched 'Erica' in 2018, evolving it into a conversational virtual assistant that also detects customer sentiment to better tailor interactions.

Exactly what occurred

Erica analyses user input, detecting frustration or confusion in chat interactions. If negative sentiment is caught, it routes users to human agents or alters its tone.

It's integrated into both the app and website, guiding users through tasks like bill pay, fraud alerts, and financial insights.

Impact

Erica has handled over 200 million client engagements, answering 80 per cent of customer questions via NLP-driven automation.[5]

17.4 Final Thoughts: How AI Tools Fit into Your Digital Marketing Strategy

Artificial Intelligence empowers you to work smarter by streamlining processes, reducing manual effort, and delivering deeper insights. With the tools mentioned in this chapter, your next step is to act with clarity and intention. Start by identifying specific challenges in your workflow—whether it's improving content quality, automating routine tasks, or making sense of data.

For example, if you often struggle with maintaining consistency across platforms, focus on AI tools that enhance coordination and quality. If analysing performance feels overwhelming, prioritize solutions that provide actionable insights to guide your decisions.

Picture this: A small marketing team with tight deadlines uses AI to simplify repetitive tasks like reporting and visual content creation. This shift gives them the bandwidth to focus on crafting a bold, creative campaign. Similarly, a solo founder can use AI to scale their efforts, turning complex strategies into manageable steps without compromising quality.

The key is to experiment, measure results, and adapt—AI works best as an extension of your expertise, amplifying what's already strong in your strategy. Think of it as a teammate, not a replacement. By integrating AI thoughtfully, you'll unlock new levels of efficiency and creativity, setting the stage for smarter, more impactful marketing.

Acknowledgements

MY HEARTFELT GRATITUDE GOES OUT TO THE MANY people who have supported me through this journey of writing the book.

First and foremost, my deepest gratitude goes to my wife, Neha, and our two daughters, Kaira and Mahiera. Thank you for your patience, love, and understanding over the past twenty-two months. Our weekends may have been consumed by this project, but your unwavering belief in me gave me the strength to see it through. I promise to make up for the lost weekends!

I am forever grateful to my mother and my entire family, whose encouragement has always been my greatest source of strength. And a special thanks to my incredible family at Kreative Machinez—thank you for holding things together with so little of my time and for giving me the space to find calm amidst the chaos. Your support made it possible for me to devote myself fully to this endeavour.

To Abhay Mishra, my mentor—thank you for your invaluable guidance. And to Poulomi, Rakshit and Asif—you guys were always there whenever I needed your time and effort.

I am also deeply thankful to my friend Gautam, who played a pivotal role by introducing me to HarperCollins. To Sachin and Shreya from the HarperCollins team—thank you for helping me shape my thoughts and bring structure to the book. I still can't believe the book is finally out! This dream wouldn't have been possible without you three.

Lastly, I bow in heartfelt gratitude to my father. Though you are no longer here physically, your words of wisdom, endless encouragement, and indomitable spirit continue to light my path. Your legacy lives on in every chapter, every sentence, and every word of this book.

Thank you all for believing in me.

Notes

Scan this QR code to access the notes.

About the Author

Pramod Maloo is the founder and head of Kreative Machinez, one of India's largest and fastest growing digital marketing agencies, serving clients across over eighteen countries, powered by a team of more than a hundred professionals. Driven by a vision to create a digitally efficient society where all businesses can thrive, Maloo established it in 2009. With over fifteen years of experience, Pramod views the internet not just as a tool, but as a bridge to boundless opportunities. For him, growth is not just a metric, it is a mindset, and his unwavering commitment to purpose, passion and presence shapes both the brands he builds and the people he inspires.

Beyond this, he has co-founded several ventures addressing real-world challenges in the digital age. Most notable ones include Sahi Hai Bazaar, a fintech platform making financial planning and wealth creation accessible to all individuals; Republic of Influencer, a marketplace connecting brands with creators; and KolkataPages.com, a pioneering initiative to bring local businesses online.

He holds an MBA from IBS Hyderabad.

Pramod's life is as dynamic as his career. He is a sought-after guest lecturer and speaker at leading B-schools, colleges and business forums, and has twice served as president of the Prudent chapter of BNI, a global networking platform, among other leadership roles. Inspired by Shah Rukh Khan, he delivered a talk—'Life Lessons from SRK'—at Pecha Kucha in 2024. Pramod has also been an integral part of the TEDx Chowringhee core team since 2022.

Maloo is a proud father to two daughters and a loving husband to his wife.

You can know more about him at pramodmaloo.com.